T0283230

Not So Sorry

Not
So Sorry

ABUSERS, FALSE APOLOGIES, AND THE LIMITS OF FORGIVENESS

Kaya Oakes

Broadleaf Books
Minneapolis

NOT SO SORRY
Abusers, False Apologies, and the Limits of Forgiveness

Portions of this book appeared as works in progress in
The Revealer, America, and Killing the Buddha.

Library of Congress Cataloging-in-Publication Data

Names: Oakes, Kaya, author.
Title: Not so sorry : abusers, false apologies, and the limits of
  forgiveness / Kaya Oakes.
Description: Minneapolis, MN : Broadleaf Books, [2024] | Includes
  bibliographical references.
Identifiers: LCCN 2023040221 (print) | LCCN 2023040222 (ebook) | ISBN
  9781506486963 (hardcover) | ISBN 9781506486970 (ebook)
Subjects: LCSH: Forgiveness--Religious aspects--Christianity. |
  Forgiveness--Psychological aspects.
Classification: LCC BV4647.F55 O36 2024 (print) | LCC BV4647.F55 (ebook) |
  DDC 234/.5--dc23/eng/20231214
LC record available at https://lccn.loc.gov/2023040221
LC ebook record available at https://lccn.loc.gov/2023040222

Cover image: © 2023 Shutterstock; Four sheets of white torn paper on a black
wall./2233761861 by Rubanitor. © 2023 Shutterstock; Wilted flower sketch.
Plant stands in a glass vase, petals crumble. Hand drawn vector illustration.
Isolated on white./2116292096 by Canatic © 2023 Shutterstock; Ink Stamp
Texture Pack Vintage Grunge Letterpress/537372098 by Inhabitant B.
Cover design: Faceout Studios

Print ISBN: 978-1-5064-8696-3
eBook ISBN: 978-1-5064-8697-0

Printed in China.

The essence of grace, we suppose, is that the account has been paid in advance; and, because it has been paid, everything can be had for nothing.

Dietrich Bonhoeffer, *The Cost of Discipleship*

Contents

Introduction

The Limits of Forgiveness

Perhaps this only makes sense if we move backward. A woman is sifting through piles of books, trying to make space for more books, which only seem to multiply with each passing year. One tumbles free from her hands, landing face-down. When she picks it up, she sees the author's name: a man she knew; an acquaintance more than a friend; a man who often put his hands on her waist and hips when they'd meet at book readings; a man who sent her messages on Facebook telling her how attractive she was; a man who won grants, teaching positions, and awards.

A couple of years before the day his book unearthed itself, complete with a signature saying something about how talented she is, she'd seen his name start repeating itself on social media. Later, a journalist would dig deeper. The word women were using was *abuser*. It went beyond touching and into emotional and physical violence, manipulation, threats. She did what you do these days with men like this and unfriended him on Facebook, and he sent her a tortured note in reply, asking why she didn't want to talk to him anymore, asking for forgiveness. A mutual acquaintance soon told her he'd received the exact same note, down to the periods and commas.

She and a different friend later get to talking and realize they have both worked for a literary organization led by a man with a habit of touching women and suggesting things to women—and as it turns out, they also know yet another man in a different literary organization who was doing the same things. All of these men are Christians, and all of them were accused, fired, and then quickly emerged and asked for forgiveness because they were "good" men—and they were apparently granted it, or they granted it to themselves, because soon they'd reappear at conferences and in literary magazines and running publishing houses. "It's just the way it works for them," she and her friends would say over and over, reading yet another email, another blog post, another tweet or message asking for forgiveness from someone who needed permission to move on.

Then there are all the ordinary things: Unwanted touches and suggestions from people who'd later ask for forgiveness. Insults or threats of violence on social media followed by notes of repentance. The everyday slights in marriage and friendship and family when one person makes mistake after mistake and the other person forgives and forgives. This person being asked for forgiveness could be me. It could be you. It could be anyone.

Trauma works backward. In the present tense, asking someone for forgiveness only takes a moment, but the sin or error can go generations deep. When a person's body or spirit or mind is violated and the violator asks to be forgiven, the wronged person must make a decision: do I do this, or not? If I do not, am I a bad person, as bad as the person who violated me? Am I just bad? Just over two thousand years ago, a thirty-three-year-old man was executed by an invading empire, and while he waited for death to take him, he asked his father to forgive the people who killed him, because they did not understand what they were doing. Because he told us that his father was God, for thousands of years since, people have felt pressured to speedily forgive anyone who has done them wrong. Trauma, however, can last years and even lifetimes. God may forgive easily, but this is less true for many of us.

Over a decade ago, I began to write about clergy abuse; spiritual abuse; and the ways in which women, children, and vulnerable populations are damaged by people in power. I did so because I saw how often the justice system, churches, and the public respond to accusations of abuse by trying to tear down the person who's been abused. We have language for this now: victim blaming. Whatever I could do to lessen the frequency of that seemed urgent.

Forgiveness, however, increasingly became part of the national conversation. It was in pop psychology, entertainment, even in sports. But mostly, forgiveness was trotted out in almost every conversation about politics and religion. In the wake of the 2015 murder of nine Black Christians in Charleston who were shot during a Bible study by a white supremacist, much of the media focus was on the miraculous notion that these people's families were somehow able to forgive Dylann Roof. In the complex legacy of slavery in America, Christianity has played the role of both oppressor and redeemer of Black people. The late theologian James Cone wrote that for Black Americans, forgiveness was a form of "deep spiritual resistance." In Cone's understanding of black liberation theology, granting others forgiveness would allow them agency, which would in turn free them from hating their oppressors. This, Cone reasoned, would ultimately be liberating. For white Americans, however, the forgiveness offered by the Charleston survivors became overrepresented to the point that the pain and anger that was also deeply felt was sometimes ignored.

I couldn't possibly say whether the forgiveness of the families was liberating for them, but the national obsession with their forgiveness sometimes felt like a racist nation's rush to absolve itself of its sins. When I went searching for sources, even the subtitle of one book about the massacre reinforced this. The journalist Jennifer Berry Hawes's otherwise excellent nonfiction account of the trial of Roof is titled *Grace Will Lead Us Home*, but the subtitle, *The Charleston Church Massacre and the Hard, Inspiring Journey to Forgiveness*, unsettled me. What is so inspiring about traumatized people feeling a pressure to forgive someone as evil and unrepentant as Roof? In her accounting of the victim statements given just forty-eight hours after the shooting, Hawes emphasizes how each person stated, "I forgive you." What she doesn't emphasize is the belief of many devout Christians that if they don't forgive, they won't go to heaven, where they believe they'd be reunited with their beloveds for eternity.

For better or worse, that notion that failing to grant forgiveness is spiritually damning has led to centuries of people being forced to turn forgiveness publicly and privately into a performance. Even for the families of the dead of Mother Emanuel, the narrative quickly became, as Hawes's book's subtitle declares, inspirational. But this is an oversimplification of what people actually said at that sentencing, which revealed deep trauma and rage. "You. Hurt. Me. You hurt a lot of people!" was shouted by Nadine Collier, the mother of one of the victims. The Reverend Anthony Thompson, husband to one of the dead, told Roof, "We would like you to take this opportunity to repent. Repent. Confess." And Felicia Sanders, whose son was dead at Roof's hands, was driven to shouting at Roof, "Every fiber in my body hurts! And I will never be the same." To listen to these voices is to hear quavering and choked-back sobs, people fighting for emotional control.

These traumatized people who had lost the people closest to them were then asked by the nation to act like they had moved past the whole thing. President Obama was reportedly so moved by the story of their ability to forgive that he based much of the eulogy he delivered for the Reverend Clementa Pickney on it. At the crescendo of his eulogy, Obama said that Roof "could have never anticipated the way the families of the fallen would respond when they saw him in court—in the midst of unspeakable grief, with words of forgiveness." This story of forgiveness replaced any kind of narrative of righteous, deserved anger, and the secondary story of what those families had to internally choke down was lost. The story of forgiveness in Charleston became so much a part of the national narrative that the writer Ta-Nehisi Coates ironically posted on Twitter that he couldn't remember "any campaign to 'love' and 'forgive' in the wake of ISIS beheadings."

We know from trauma theory that expecting victims to repeatedly revisit the scenes of their abuse means they are being re-traumatized each time that happens, often for the sake of abusers who would like to be forgiven so they can move on. In early 2022, Dylann Roof fired his attorneys when they tried to argue he was suffering from mental illness, signaling that he remains unrepentant. In his manifesto, Roof had written that he had "no choice" other than to kill Black people due to his fear of Black on white crime. Roof, who claimed to have read "hundreds" of slave narratives, argued that they all portrayed enslaved people as content, further adding to the distorted idea that Black people were naturally submissive to whites. And a submissive person is, of course, assumed to be forgiving.

But it is unclear whether Roof was aware that one of the founders of Mother Emanuel was Denmark Vesey. Vesey, a former enslaved person who had bought his freedom with lottery winnings, was also a lay preacher at Emanuel. It was there that Vesey's influence grew and where he began to plot a slave rebellion that would have led to thousands of enslaved Black people rising up, killing their masters, and fleeing to Haiti, which in the early 1800s had defeated

Napoleon and become a free Black republic. But Vesey's rebellion was crushed, and he was hanged alongside dozens of others who had hoped to free thousands of enslaved people. Mother Emanuel was founded by rebels, and slave rebellions were driven by righteous indignation, not by submission and forgiveness.

But Vesey's rebellion was rarely if ever mentioned in the story of the Charleston nine. As an American, my historical education was spotty and distorted by mandated curriculums. It was only as an adult and far past both college and graduate school that these pieces of American history began to fall into place. They particularly did so in the past decade, as Black Americans have become increasingly vocal about their refusal to forgive a nation that has nurtured people like Dylann Roof, George Zimmerman, and the police officers who have killed Black people. As a white American, I can never know what it is like to see this kind of news story repeated over and over again. But I can recognize when something seems unforgivable.

As a feminist, I also have concerns that women in particular are increasingly asked to perform their trauma, sometimes in ways that feel queasily exploitative, similar to the ways the Catholic Church has venerated and set as examples the goriest and most disturbing stories of women saints. And women are often asked to do this so that a man can be forgiven. As a person who grew up surrounded by the Bay Area's queer community and remembers the furious and effective pressure that community put on the medical establishment during the worst of the AIDS epidemic, when thousands of people around the Bay Area were sick and dying, that unforgiving rage made sense. In my friends' lives with AIDS and in their deaths, I also saw the pressure to forgive doctors, politicians, and friends and family who refused to care about a "gay plague."

In my own position as a straight, white, educated woman, I can only try to understand what it means when a person from a minority community is asked to forgive. But I'm also aware that 81 percent of women experience sexual violence or sexual harassment, and I know how that trauma lives in the mind and body well past the time of the event. I, too, have been abused and asked to forgive, and I have not always been able to grant forgiveness. I am also tired of hearing that this makes me or anyone else a bad person.

As a person baptized into the Roman Catholic Church of her family as an infant, who has remained in that church despite its egregious abuses of power and repeated failures to make amends, many of which have been revealed only in recent decades, this, too, has sometimes strained my ability to forgive. The decision and negotiation that millions of people experience of choosing to stay affiliated with problematic institutions in hopes of influencing them to change is one that this book will also explore because those institutions have historically mishandled the issue of forgiveness, which for many of us is tied up in the negotiations about choosing to stay and hoping to be an agent of change, or choosing to go because change can seem impossible.

In fact, when I first began to write about the topic of forgiveness, I did it at the behest of a Catholic magazine that had asked me to explore the idea of how women should handle it when men asked them for forgiveness in the wake of the #MeToo movement.

Spending a few months researching, arguing, and negotiating with that topic was not an insubstantial investment of time and mental energy. It seemed like an important conversation that readers needed to have.

The magazine declined to publish the essay. Their argument was that the central idea of the essay—that forgiveness has limits, that it can become a form of spiritual abuse, and that we need to move to a victim-centered approach in our understanding of it—was antithetical to the message of Jesus. In their interpretation, our command as Christians is to forgive everyone for everything, no matter what. But the problem with the idea that Jesus was asking people to forgive those who abuse them is that it is not necessarily a correct interpretation of Scripture. Jesus asked us to forgive those who know *not* what they do. But what do we do about the people who knew exactly what they were doing?

Christians have not always been willing to examine the idea that forgiveness is meted out not by the judicial system, with its mythologies of checks and balances, or by centralized institutions like the Vatican, but by the person who was violated. The onus for forgiving, repeatedly, is laid at the feet of the victim. What are perpetrators really asking victims to do? To absolve them. When Catholics make confession, we are told to "go and sin no more." But it is abundantly clear that abusers do not always follow this command. Meanwhile, the victims are left behind to grapple with the repercussions of the abuse.

Sexual harassment and sexual violence in particular tend to occur in a serial manner, one violation after another, on and on, until someone has enough of the silencing and speaks out. Then come the apologies, so many apologies, riddled with "but" and "however" and "although I recall things differently." Since the #MeToo floodgates opened, we have been offered a series of apologies. Many abusers do not explicitly ask for forgiveness but they sometimes acknowledge the damage they have done. And in that, even in our secular era, there is an implied request for repentance and absolution.

We Christians would like to pretend that we understand what forgiveness means. We march into confessionals to be forgiven. Us Catholics recite the Confiteor every Sunday, where we ask the congregation to forgive us. We have Lent and Advent, entire liturgical seasons focused on penitence. Jesus's own words about forgiveness from Luke are drilled into our catechesis: "Even if they sin against you seven times in a day and seven times come back saying 'I repent,' you must forgive them." And on Good Friday, we hear Jesus pleading with God to forgive his killers "who know not what they do." Evangelicals also believe that forgiveness must always be granted and that sins can be absolved with a simple prayer. But this can lead to the very concept of forgiveness itself being abused.

Abusers will emphasize this: they knew not what they did. "I was drunk. I understood the situation differently. I assumed it was consensual. My recollection is different." In the context of serial abusers like Larry Nassar or in the horrors of slavery or the American Indian genocide, Christ's emphasis on forgiving no matter how many times someone sins against us is nearly impossible to comprehend. Many of Nassar's victims were too young to understand they were being sexually violated. They took years to come forward because it took years for them to understand that what happened to them was deeply sick and wrong.

For Catholics, the topic of abuse remains a painful one. The church's failure to rectify its abusive history, which has caused harm not only to the people abused and their families but to the church as a whole, has also resulted in the hemorrhaging of laypeople out of the church in addition to shrinking numbers of seminarians and suspicious attitudes toward clergy. Surveys have suggested as many as half of former Catholics point to the abuse crisis as a primary reason for leaving the church. More recently, abuse coverups on a massive scale in the Southern Baptist Convention have come to light alongside abuse stories from almost every mainline Protestant denomination and in Evangelical megachurches like Hillsong. Informal conversations with still-practicing Christians often reveal unresolved feelings of betrayal and anger about abuse, which feels like an open wound.

More significantly, abuse has also left a trail of traumatized victims, many of whom are still suffering from physical, psychological, and spiritual damage. Spiritual damage, which often means damage to a person's religious faith or relationship with God, is probably the least discussed and least well understood of these issues. The lack of understanding of what spiritual abuse can do to people whose religious faith is important to their lives may in fact be the reason why spiritual abuse is so pervasive. And forcing someone to forgive can become a form of spiritual abuse.

Yet the heart of Christian faith is still a message of forgiveness. But in a time when the sins of Christian institutions are revealed almost constantly, are those institutions really deserving of forgiveness? Even as I wrote this introduction, a prominent German cardinal became one of the first church authorities to tender his resignation for failing to resolve the abuse crisis. A statue of a racist Civil War leader was finally removed from Charlottesville, three years after white supremacists marched through the city, three years after city leaders asked for forgiveness when a racist drove into the crowd and killed a woman protesting for Black lives. And a well-known member of the Southern Baptist Coalition also stepped down from his position, calling out the denomination's pattern of silencing abusers along the way. All of them asked for forgiveness. Who will grant it? And what forgiveness are they really owed? These are the questions this book will explore, in the hope of creating new understandings about what forgiveness really means.

1

Fetishizing Forgiveness

What It Is, and Who It's For

House cats may spend most of their days asleep, but when they're awake, if you've got more than one of them, they're highly likely to fight. Competition in the natural world for food and territory may be a far cry from a domesticated cat's comfortable life of puffy sofas and daily, regular feedings, but animals still feel a need to battle it out. At a dog park, you'll see the same thing: barking and chasing. But no matter the species, even if they bite hard enough to draw blood, animals—at least, animals who are part of the same pack, the same herd, or the same species—usually seem to forgive one another.

Anyone who's sat through a nature documentary knows there are exceptions. Sometimes animals who are part of the same community fight to the death for a mate, sometimes over territory.

But more typically, fights end quickly, and the herd goes back to grazing, hunting, or just surviving. Sometimes animals become enemies for life, an unfortunate reality for some pet owners. But they mostly just go back to being compatible or, at the worst, ignoring one another.

This kind of forgiveness may not be what we think about in the larger scope of conversations about what forgiveness means. But our hominid ancestors lived in tribes, and for better or worse, we are still animals. The behavior of moving past a conflict made our survival as a species possible because we usually learned how to stop fighting before we beat one another to death. In any competition for survival, a pack is more likely to survive than a solitary animal. So it could be argued that in the role forgiveness plays in community solidarity, it is probably hardwired into our DNA.

Yet one of the reasons we evolved as a species from swimming to crawling to walking is because we were willing to override this primitive form of forgiveness in our genetic code. We learned to forgive in order to protect the pack, but we also learned when a pack member could not be forgiven. In those same nature documentaries, you might recall the solitary animal, cast out on its own, wandering the wilderness. That is the unforgiven animal. Later we also learned to forgive those outside of our pack, which helped civilizations to grow. But with that came increased conflict. And revenge or retribution might be as deeply embedded in our genes as forgiveness. Any visit to Twitter or the comment box on an article will remind us that we seek conflict as often as we seek compatibility.

But what do we really mean when we talk about forgiveness? The understanding most of us have is that forgiveness is essentially a kind of moral gift granted to us, even if we don't deserve it, or to someone who has wronged us, even if they don't ask for it. There's also a common notion that we somehow "forgive and forget," moving past harm and leaving it behind, which is often far from our lived reality. Forgiveness is often portrayed as salvific, something that will help a person turn their life around. It's depicted as a virtue in every religious tradition. Muslims refer to Allah as "Ghafir," or all-forgiving. In the Dharmic religions of Buddhism, Hinduism, and Jainism, seeking forgiveness is an important step toward both mental clarity and cultivating compassion. Judaism's focus on atonement is so paramount that many of the Yom Kippur prayers are based on this.

Christianity, however, is what shaped much of Western thinking about forgiveness, and nearly every classic work of literature, film, theater, and music made by Christian or lapsed Christian artists has involved some portrayal of forgiveness. In America in particular, our collective imagination is shaped by the idea that forgiveness is a virtue and failing to forgive is vice, sin, and failure.

There are thousands of examples of depictions of people learning to forgive and becoming saintly as a result. In Tolstoy's *War and Peace*, the central love triangle between Andrei, Natasha, and Pierre hinges on Andrei's movement from unforgiving to forgiving. Initially, he finds himself unable to forgive his fiancée Natasha when she's seduced by a sleazy aristocrat. But his friend Pierre helps him to understand that Natasha is a victim, and Andrei eventually comes to forgive her. Tolstoy, a spiritual seeker throughout his life and a practitioner of an idiosyncratic, anarchic vision of Christianity that got him excommunicated from the Russian Orthodox church, was a strong moralist in his fiction. Andrei's arc from unforgiving to forgiving is moving because Tolstoy helps us to believe that Andrei's redemption is necessary for Natasha's.

Tolstoy's understanding of forgiveness and that of much classical literature depicting forgiveness, from *Les Miserables* to *A Chistmas Carol*, however, predates modern psychology. Up until the twentieth century, when psychology evolved into how it's practiced today, how people understood forgiveness was rooted more in philosophy and religion. And both of those continue to influence how we talk about forgiveness today. In essence, our understanding of forgiveness often lands in the middle of a Venn diagram of philosophy, psychology, and religion. Plato and Aristotle, the founders of Western philosophy, saw controlling anger as important to leading a virtuous life and understood forgiveness as a route toward freeing a person from anger. But as Christianity evolved and conquered, forgiveness itself became virtue, and failing to forgive became vice.

The diametric opposite of forgiveness is revenge. And depictions of revenge can be a highly enjoyable way for us to live out the fantasy that we might get our own revenge instead of being forgiving. In the 2022 film *The Banshees of Innisherin*, a conflict between old friends escalates to absurdist levels of violence as the two men trade acts of revenge. At the end of the film, Pádraic, whose house has been burned down by his former friend Colm, says, "some things there's no moving on from, and I think that's a good thing." In 2020's *Promising Young Woman*, a former medical student whose friend was raped by a classmate systematically takes revenge on everyone from the school who colluded to cover it up. In 2002's *Oldboy*, a man freed from prison after many years for reasons he doesn't understand sets out on a series of acts of revenge, and even 1980's feminist classic comedy *9 to 5* is about a group of women getting their revenge on their misogynistic boss. And this is just a random sampling from a much bigger genre stretching back thousands of years of art depicting revenge.

These movies are enjoyable because they're a kind of wish fulfillment. Instead of being forgiving, the characters get what most of us really want deep down inside when we've been wronged, which is to hurt the person who did it. Sublimating that instinct for revenge is one of the great battles of our lives. The difference between us and our barking, snarling house pets is that we keep thinking about being wronged long past the event itself, sometimes for years or even centuries. Revenge fantasies are an escape from the reality that forgiving is sometimes just more pragmatic. But the fact is that while forgiving one another may be part of what keeps our world from tumbling into violence, it is not always as easy as we're taught to think. And it is not always possible for the wronged, the wrongdoer, or their community.

While many portrayals of forgiveness focus on reconciliation, with the offender being welcomed back into a relationship or a group, modern philosophers like Jean Hampton have argued that reconciliation can be "morally unwise." If the offending party doesn't recognize what they've done as wrong, offering forgiveness can put the victim in a more vulnerable position. This is closely related to cycles of abuse in domestic and institutional relationships. If a victim is always forgiving, the offending person essentially is given permission to keep doing wrong. A tendency to rush to forgiveness can also indicate a lack of self-respect because the individual who does this may struggle to understand that sometimes forgiveness isn't actually owed. And if most acts of forgiveness are private and internal, the offending person may not even be aware of them and will just keep on doing wrong.

Some philosophers also argue that forgiveness cannot work unless it comes with conditions. Charles Griswold, from Boston University, writes that forgiveness is not unlimited and that it is the wrongdoer who is responsible for fulfilling the conditions for forgiveness. In Griswold's argument, the perpetrator must acknowledge they've done wrong, repudiate what they've done, express regret, commit to change, show they understand the damage they've done, and explain why they did wrong in the first place.

But even if reconciliation isn't always possible, philosophically, as Griswold says, "reconciliation is the goal to which forgiveness points." The animal kingdom example works again here. The pack is stronger when its members are reconciled. It will survive. The same can be argued for nations struggling to move past painful episodes in their histories. South Africa's Truth and Reconciliation Commission, which shed a global light on the atrocities of apartheid, worked to demonstrate that unless those atrocities were made public, reconciliation would never really be possible and the nation would never really be unified. Bishop Desmond Tutu, a member of that commission, was clearly influenced by the words of Jesus from the Gospel of Luke: "For nothing is hidden that will not be disclosed, nor is anything secret that will not become known and come to light."

Divine forgiveness, however, can be difficult to grasp and explain. Who can really know the mind of God? If forgiveness is in God's hands, as Jesus says on the cross, how do we know when or if God has forgiven us? Christian theologians beginning with the apostle Paul have made claims about the conditions under which God's forgiveness takes place, but the existential truth is that we can't and don't truly know. We can only assume that some combination of atonement, right behavior, amends, and apology will get us close enough for God to grant us forgiveness. In Catholicism, the priest, acting "in persona Christi," does the forgiving on God's behalf in the sacrament of reconciliation, more commonly known as confession. But forgiveness in confession always comes with penance of some sort, or else it's understood that it doesn't work. And in American Evangelical theology, forgiveness can be as simple as a sinner's prayer or surrendering your life to Jesus.

There is also a performative kind of repentance and forgiveness, where a person asks for forgiveness but is essentially unchanged when granted it. If forgiveness means moving past and letting go of resentment toward someone who's wronged you, as many philosophers and psychologists agree, that assumes that the person being forgiven is actively working to avoid making the same mistake again. This, of course, is far from reality in many cases. Philosopher Richard Swinburne writes that "forgiving in the performative sense consists in deeming the wrongdoer's atonement sufficient," which implies that the person doing the forgiving assumes that there's a promise inherent to forgiveness. It is the promise that the person who did wrong is working to become a better person. However, Swinburne continues, "Just as no one has any obligation to forgive, so no one has any obligation to treat the wrongdoer who does not repent as one who has wronged them."

Forgiveness, in many ways, can become reflexive and therefore a rote performance of repentance. If we assume that the person asking for it won't harm us again, we can say we forgive without really thinking about the implications. As a woman, I was brought up understanding that apologizing for every minor thing from bumping into someone to tripping over a manspreader on the train was a way to avoid making men angry. But men just kept getting angry no matter how much I apologized. The submissive requests for forgiveness became a performance of an idea of womanhood rather than a concerted effort to get men to stop being angry all the time.

Most psychologists today believe that forgiveness is both interpersonal and intrapersonal. It is, in other words, both internal and external, something that happens between people to accomplish a social outcome and something that happens inside a person's own mind, thoughts, and emotions. Thus, a certain degree of performance is always going to be involved in interpersonal forgiveness because we usually let the other person know that we've forgiven them when they ask to be forgiven. The internal process of deciding to grant forgiveness, however, is so individualistic that it would be impossible to sum it up without being reductive. What we can do instead is look at how psychologists understand this process, see how it works in real-life relationships, and understand when our thought process might instead lead us to decide not to forgive someone.

But who is forgiveness really for? In philosophy, religion, art, and literature, forgiveness is often depicted as liberating for the person who has done wrong. But modern psychologists have begun to focus instead on the idea that forgiving is really about liberating the person offering the forgiveness from resentment, anger, or a desire for revenge. If holding on to grief or pain can lead to resentment, which can be psychologically damaging, forgiving someone could theoretically be an end to that resentment. In this framing, it's the person doing the forgiving who benefits the most.

The psychologist Fred Luskin, who formerly ran Stanford University's Forgiveness Project, says that learning to grant forgiveness is a way of understanding that being told "no" is a universal experience. For example, you may want your spouse to be faithful, but they aren't, so you get "no" as a response to your desires. You want someone to tell you the truth, but they lie, so you get "no." According to Luskin, "the essence of forgiveness is being resilient when things don't go the way you want," and learning to accept that things are not always going to go like we want them to is a key to moving past resentment and into forgiveness.

But Luskin acknowledges that you can't forgive someone without grieving. When someone does us wrong, we have to recognize that our relationship is forever changed, and we have to grieve that change. Instead of letting go of the experience, Luskin says allowing ourselves to grieve helps us transform our emotional response to it, which can help us to become more resilient and more forgiving. And he also writes that not hiding the process you're experiencing is crucial. Research has shown that people who experience trauma and don't share that experience have worse outcomes than those who do. Sharing an experience of trauma, for many people, means spending time dwelling in sadness, anger, or anguish, not necessarily moving quickly to forgiveness. Perhaps forgiveness is good for trauma survivors, but so is making room for emotions that are not forgiving. And we must remember that forgiveness is a process, one that may be most beneficial for both victims and wrongdoers when it's an open process rather than a hidden one. This may be why sexual abuse victims in particular find it so difficult to arrive at forgiveness, since shame and secrecy are inherent to many cases of sexual abuse.

The former pope Benedict XVI died while I was writing this book, and the knowledge that he had failed to act to end sex abuse by priests in Germany while he was an archbishop undergirded every word of praise I saw lavished on him in obituaries and on social media. Children were raped while he stood by and did nothing. Why were people so forgiving of a person who'd colluded to allow that to happen? Because this abuse was so shameful, it had stayed a secret until he retired from the papacy and wasn't made public until the year he died. Among the eulogies praising his theological mind and his love of music and art, the voices of abuse victims were hardly heard at all. It's very likely they had not forgiven him—worse, that many of them had never shared their trauma, had never grieved what had been done to them.

If psychologists argue that learning to forgive benefits the person who's been wronged because it allows them to move past resentment and revenge fantasies and into a freedom from mental burdens, the problem is that memories of a traumatic event can last for the rest of a person's life. Sex abuse victims have talked extensively about this, as have war veterans, cult survivors, and many other people whose bodies and minds have been violated. Post-traumatic stress disorder, or PTSD, is characterized by flash-backs and recurring nightmares returning a person to a traumatic event. While PTSD can be treated, like many other mental health conditions, it can't necessarily be cured in the way a physical disease sometimes can, where the symptoms are vanquished for good. A person who has done wrong isn't necessarily trapped in a hellish loop in the same way the person they damaged is. It's possible that PTSD means a person cannot forgive because the memories are so deeply embedded in their psyche.

Another side of PTSD is moral injury, a term psychiatrists and psychologists use to describe what happens to a person who acts against their beliefs or witnesses acts that go against their beliefs. The US Department of Veterans Affairs describes moral injury as "the distressing psychological, behavioral, social, and sometimes spiritual aftermath of exposure to such events." Moral injury closely overlaps with PTSD but often has a spiritual or religious dimen-sion as well. It's also often intertwined with guilt and shame, which can lead a person to keep traumatic events secret. In other words, a person suffering from moral injury is not in an ideal position to offer forgiveness.

One study by psychiatrists looks at examples of people suffering from moral injury being led through "forgiveness practices" with spiritual or religious leaders. For example, a veteran of the Afghanistan conflict dealing with PTSD met a psychologist who recognized the veteran's guilt over killing people was an example of moral injury. The vet, who was deeply religious, was unable to forgive God for what had happened, so he met with a religious leader who led him through a series of reconciliation exercises that helped the vet forgive his chain of command and, eventually, forgive God. This seems like a powerful example of forgiveness actually working. But it also stands in contrast to unknown thousands of veterans who struggle with substance abuse, suicidality, and violence because they were asked to fight and kill on someone else's behalf. The loss of personal agency in war means it is a challenge to understand who exactly veterans are supposed to forgive and how they are supposed to do it.

When it comes to people who are not able to forgive, some psychologists argue that this may be a way of protecting themselves from further harm. Psychologist Jeanne Safer, the author of *Forgiving and Not Forgiving*, argues that "enshrining universal forgiveness as a panacea, a requirement or the only moral choice, is rigid, simplistic and even pernicious." Yet, according to Safer, we've come to expect forgiveness to be granted so universally that we demonize anyone unwilling to grant it. The problem here is that we equate forgiveness with a kind of moral purity that very few people can live up to. In her reading, there are many cases when not forgiving someone is the most appropriate action to take.

For the people Safer refers to as moral unforgivers—those who withhold forgiveness for moral reasons—refusing to forgive means telling the truth, asserting fundamental rights, and opposing injustice. Psychologically detached unforgivers accept the painful reality that they cannot experience any positive internal connection with a betrayer, which forgiving would require. Reformed forgivers—those who have forgiven people and later regretted it—have faced conflicts between feelings, religious principles, ethics, or social responsibilities and come to reject the conventional attitudes they once accepted. But none of these three types of people is vindictive or against forgiveness in principle. They share the capacity to forgive but have come to a decision that in certain cases, forgiveness, rather than freeing them from patterns of negative thinking, can further damage them psychologically.

In Safer's telling, this decision not to forgive can sometimes be liberating for the children of abusive parents. This doesn't mean those people necessarily cut off all communication or refuse to acknowledge a parent but that they are "outraged but not obsessed" by the harm done to them. When people insist on universal forgiveness, it can blind them to the fact that reconciliation without forgiveness is not only possible but can also provide closure. It is, of course, also easier to forgive an abusive or neglectful parent when that person has died. My friend Katya's father was an alcoholic, and this led to a series of cascading health issues that eventually caused his death. Before he died, he showed up to drive her home from school so drunk he couldn't see straight, was sometimes verbally abusive toward her mother and siblings, and was emotionally volatile.

However, it took Katya decades to understand that she could reconcile with her father's behavior without forgiving it. He had an inherited disease, and he refused to get treatment for it. His own father had also died from drinking, and it's likely this impacted generations in his family. It's not possible to forgive someone's DNA, and she couldn't forgive his refusal to acknowledge what he was doing to his body and mind. Instead, she chose to live with the understanding that even if she didn't forgive him, she was allowed to miss him and to wish he had turned his bad habits around.

Proponents of universal forgiveness would likely argue that in cases like Katya's, refusing to forgive her father means that she will never be able to heal or move on. But years and years of therapy have helped her to understand that this is not necessarily the case. This is also true for my friend Mary. Mary's father was also an alcoholic, and when he died, one of her sisters took all of their father's money, and the other one came to the funeral so drunk she was falling down. When Mary decided to cut ties with her sisters, their mother would not stop telling her to forgive them. Eventually, the alcoholic sister drank herself to death, at which point Mary's mother, a devout Catholic, told Mary she was angry about the whole situation and wanted to talk to her about it. But Mary's mother had never allowed Mary to be angry or to express any of the rage and frustration she felt about her family's behavior. Mary, realizing they would never be able to come to any agreement about this, told her mother to go talk to a priest about it. Mary struggled for many years deciding whether to forgive her father for drinking; her sisters for stealing his money and also falling into alcoholism; and her mother for insisting everyone bury their emotions. She says she feels somewhat guilty about not forgiving her father for refusing to acknowledge his alcoholism, but that she's at peace with her decision to be a moral unforgiver in the case of her sisters. To stay in contact would only perpetuate the dysfunction, possibly be mistaken for forgiveness, and would likely worsen Mary's own feelings about her family's unwillingness to change.

Mary is Christian, and her faith makes her what some people would describe as "deeply religious." She is also politically progressive and doesn't necessarily subscribe to orthodoxy when it comes to her faith, but she tries to take the gospels seriously in how she treats other people. And yet, because she's not really able to forgive, some of her fellow Christians have told her that this is the most unchristian thing she could do. For some children of alcoholics, however, being overly forgiving would also mean that they might be less likely to say something when a friend, partner, or child is drinking too heavily and refusing to talk about it. Deciding that they don't forgive an alcoholic parent can also allow them to decide to hold themselves accountable. In order to avoid the very thing that caused a parent to lose control and die, many of them refuse to become alcoholics themselves. It can also help them to define what forgiveness means for themselves and to consider what outcomes being forgiving of an addictive parent would bring about. If they'd forgiven their parent for being an alcoholic and failing to do anything about it, it's not unlikely that they might argue that hard drinking is in their genes and give themselves permission to take it up again.

The pandemic has also revealed fault lines in our understanding of forgiveness. In the most recent season of the podcast *Serial*, the poet Rachel McKibbens tells the story of how her father and brother both died from COVID-19 just a few weeks apart. Her father, who had been physically abusive to her and her brother throughout their childhood, still displayed qualities that caused both Rachel and her brother Peter to stay in touch with him as adults. Their father took them in when their mother put them in foster care. He supported Rachel's interest in acting and theater and drove her to rehearsals all over the Los Angeles area. He loved movies and watched them with his kids and was scrupulous about making sure they always had the same amount of food. But he drank, and when he drank, he got violent. Rachel and her brother, like many children of abusive and alcoholic parents, became a team, paired up against their father's rage.

When Rachel grew up, she married, had five kids, and moved across the country. But her brother seems to have gotten stuck, both emotionally and physically. He moved back in with his father and tried and failed to get him to stop drinking. Rachel says Peter became "really sort of like this parent," cooking, cleaning, and looking after his dad. But when COVID-19 hit, both father and son refused to get vaccinated. They began to tunnel down rabbit holes of conspiracy theories about vaccines and the government, fueled by texts from a cousin whose messages Rachel discovered after they had both passed away. Her father refused to go to the hospital when he got COVID-19, and he died at home. Shortly after, Peter's health rapidly declined as well. Peter believed both of them got COVID-19 from a different cousin at a family funeral, a cousin who was vaccinated, because one of the online conspiracies about COVID-19 is that vaccinated people "shed" the virus and give it to unvaccinated people. Peter could not forgive this vaccinated cousin.

Instead, Peter became obsessed with the advice he was getting from the antivaccination cousin, and as his own COVID-19 case got worse and he became feverish and short of breath, he called his sister. Rachel told him, "If you don't go to the E.R. right now, I will not forgive you when you die." Peter went to the E.R., where he was put on oxygen, but he refused medication due to the conspiracy theory that doctors are paid to give medication to COVID-19 patients. He told his sister he was released because he was getting better, but this was a lie. He discharged himself against medical advice, went home, and died. He was 44 years old, didn't drink or smoke, and lifted weights.

Three years into the pandemic, there are millions of stories like this. Rachel says she herself feels she needs forgiveness for not pushing her father and brother harder to get vaccinated, but at some point, when a person refuses to get help, even to get something as simple as a safe and effective vaccine, they move past being seen as forgivable and into a messier, grayer area where only those closest to them can make that choice. This story also reminds us that sometimes we have to decide whether or not to forgive people for hurting themselves. When that decision has emotional consequences for others, however, it reminds us that sometimes deciding not to forgive someone is a form of taking back control.

For marginalized groups, an unwillingness to forgive can be useful for creating social change or protecting the community.

During the AIDS epidemic, millions of people were abandoned by their parents and families because they were considered untouchable. But it was enraged, unrelenting, and one might say *unforgiving* pressure from gay men, at that time most at risk of contracting the disease, that pushed the American government into funding medical research and pushed medical companies into making those lifesaving drugs affordable and accessible. Some of those same men who survived AIDS never forgave or reconciled with the families that rejected them. Today, untold numbers of queer and trans kids are also rejected by their families of origin, and they struggle to feel forgiving. But if they can't bring themselves to forgive those parents, does that make them bad people? I know far too many people who fit these descriptions who cannot forgive their parents for rejecting them and have had to self-create families that are more understanding and supportive. In no case would I describe them as "bad." They are, in fact, some of the most truly empathetic and compassionate people I've ever known.

Perhaps, for some people, forgiveness can be freeing. But in cases where it would do further damage, enable abuse, or cause someone to engage in self-harm, forgiveness can do the opposite. It can put us into a moral cage of "goodness" where we become trapped by the idea that failing to forgive means we are fundamentally bad people. And this is particularly true among Christians in America. Decades of the rise of fundamentalist thinking about Christianity have led people to believe that Jesus always preached forgiveness, that he demanded it, and that failing to give it makes you a bad Christian and even an apostate.

But the gospel stories of forgiveness are not that simplistic. They are complicated, they must be framed by historical context to make sense, and they are often oversimplified and distorted by millennia of mistranslations and poor theological thinking. American Christian ideas of forgiveness are also shaped by our country's history of predestination, manifest destiny, slavery, colonialism, misogyny, homophobia, and many other social ills that have become deeply intertwined with Christian religion. These ideas that forgiveness must be universal are cross-denominational, too, impacting every American Christian from Catholics to Protestants, from overwhelmingly white Mormons to Black Christians who belong to churches founded by formerly enslaved people.

Just as our nation both insists it believes in the separation of church and state and insists lawmakers take an oath of office with one hand on a holy book, we fetishize forgiveness to the point of insisting on it—yet in many concrete ways, we are among the least forgiving societies in the world. Our rate of incarceration is among the world's highest. The death penalty is legal in twenty-seven states, and according to the Prison Policy Initiative, nearly two million children and adults are locked up in America today. Families trying to cross the border into America, who are often fleeing abuse, violence, and death, are put into cages and detention centers where they lack adequate food, medicine, and water, then they're sent back home to suffer and die. And a woman seeking an abortion because she's been raped or is a victim of incest will be unable to get one in thirteen states as of this writing, and likely many more in the future. We are not a forgiving nation.

In America, forgiveness is closely tied up with power. Culturally powerful people demonize and refuse to forgive the culturally weak, all the while demanding that the weak forgive the powerful without preconditions. The homeless crisis is a perfect illustration of this dichotomy. Unhoused people are vilified and blamed for their homelessness, when the erosion of social services for the mentally ill, addicted, and poor forces more and more people into a life on the streets. And yet, the unhoused are also supposed to feel forgiving when a tent city is bulldozed or their goods are seized. Powerful people could help solve the homeless crisis. But instead, they focus on blaming homeless people for being homeless, while also insisting those same homeless people forgive them for denying the homeless even a sidewalk to sleep on. In many cities, buildings are surrounded by spikes, fences, and security guards just to keep someone from sleeping outside. And those same people are expected to forgive the people who erect these boundaries.

I'm not against forgiveness. Forgiveness can indeed be liberating. It can mend relationships, heal emotional wounds, and make us feel better about ourselves. But expecting universal forgiveness can also enable abuse. It can cause self-harm. It can lead to suicide and addiction. It can also drive people away from religion when religion makes them feel like failures for being unable to forgive. Forgiveness is something that should improve our lives and our society, but America today is a stellar example of why this is very much not the case. It will take a collective willingness to pick apart some of our own preconceptions to understand how we got here, and how we might reframe our understanding of forgiveness to see that it has limits and that we sometimes need them.

2

Seventy Times Seven

The Limits of Christian Understandings of Forgiveness

If we want to talk about forgiveness, we have to begin with sin. Without sin, there's no need for forgiveness. The fall must come before salvation, otherwise no one would need to be saved. Our understandings of forgiveness, particularly in America, are often this simplistic. A person errs, asks for forgiveness, is granted it, and moves on. And this can be traced back to our roots as a nation that was founded by people with a version of Christianity rooted in a vision of humanity's extreme sinfulness. People in Plymouth Colony were put to death, whipped, sent to the stocks, and fined for everything from theft to bestiality to killing to "buggery" to accusations of witchcraft. And the Bible was often used to justify both those accusations and their punishments.

During the Salem witch trials, the fever pitch of Puritan accusations became so high the jails were overflowing, and even the wife of Massachusetts's governor was accused of being a witch. Samuel Sewall, a merchant who was appointed to a court that investigated witchcraft accusations, eventually saw the scale of accusations grow to such frenzied heights and stretches of the imagination that eventually even the judge presiding over the court resigned in disgust. Sewall was so horrified by the scale of the Puritan thirst for punishment and wracked with guilt for his part in it that he suggested the entire colony spend a day fasting and praying for forgiveness. Sewall said he would "take the blame and shame" for the trials, and he asked both God and his fellow congregants to forgive him.

As with most of history, there's a frustrating blank in our understanding of how Sewall felt when he asked for forgiveness. Alongside the idea of granting forgiveness being good for the soul of the forgiver, there is also a Christian notion that *asking* for forgiveness frees us, that we are liberated from sin by forgiveness and given the "clean slate" that enables us to move on with our lives, unfettered by guilt. Perhaps Sewall felt better when he asked for forgiveness. Perhaps Sewall's fellow colonists really did believe that offering prayers earned them absolution for the deaths they caused. But the people whose lives they were responsible for ending were the ones unable to do any forgiving. Only the living can forgive. The dead, in their silence, can only condemn.

Like many Americans, my own family's religion was shaped by colonialism and immigration. The Irish Catholicism of my ancient ancestors, with its mishmash of pre-Christian symbolism, Celtic mythology, and Gaelic language, was swept away by the arrival of the English, who effectively destroyed the Irish language and tried to scrub the church of any pagan and Druidic notions. When those same ancestors arrived in America, they brought their superstitions and rituals with them, but much like the Puritans before them, they also brought something that often arises from living under an oppressive rule: an obsession with sin. The Catholic Church in America encouraged this as a way of keeping people in line, a mental colonization that has impacted generations descended from immigrant families from all over the world.

Sin casts a long shadow over how I learned about forgiveness. Early catechesis in my childhood emphasized two ideas about sin rooted in the church's patriarchal thinking: that we were all born with it because of Eve and that only a male priest could forgive us through the sacrament of confession and reconciliation. From a feminist point of view, there are layers of obvious problems with these ideas, but like many other Catholic kids, as I grew older, my evolving understanding of sinfulness came from a confusing mixture of inherited Irish Catholic guilt (everything is sinful) and growing up in a politically progressive part of the United States among mostly nonreligious people (nothing is sinful). In the exhausted, half-baked catechesis delivered by burned-out nuns and underpaid teachers in my youth, Jesus told us sin was bad, and if you did something bad to someone else, you asked for forgiveness because you obviously wanted to be like Jesus. The end.

Catholicism was so interested in sin it eventually divided sins into two categories, venial and mortal. Of the venial ones, as a child

I was taught these were the basics, like refusing to share things with my younger sister or talking back to my parents. The mortal sins were the biggies, like murder, but strangely also missing Mass on Sundays was sometimes venial and sometimes mortal depending on the mood of the priest you got for confession. But almost nobody was going to confession by the time I was old enough to have my first one, a mortifying 1970s experiment called "public confession" where you had to confess your sins in front of your entire giggling, gasping classroom.

Hamartiology, the branch of theology dedicated to the study of the concept of sin, is closely tied to Christian ideas of ethics and morals. The early church fathers, like Saint Augustine, wrote extensively about sinfulness—in Augustine's case, to a degree we might see today as scrupulosity, a psychological disorder where the person is obsessed with moral issues to a dysfunctional degree. For Augustine, who believed sin was a human creation, even something as banal as stealing pears from a neighbor's tree becomes the occasion for operatic levels of guilt in *The Confessions,* written around the year 400 CE:

> Now, behold, let my heart tell Thee what it sought there, that I should be gratuitously evil, having no temptation to ill, but the ill itself. It was foul, and I loved it; I loved to perish, I loved mine own fault, not that for which I was faulty, but my fault itself.

Augustine's thinking about sin as a choice, and a very tempting one, would go on to influence centuries of church teaching. Later in the

Confessions, Augustine would similarly sinfully writhe around in his descriptions of his sexual relationship with his unnamed concubine, the mother of his child, although he seems less guilt-ridden when he abandons them to become a priest and later a bishop than he was about those stolen pears.

But it was St. Thomas Aquinas who would finesse the understanding of sins in his *Summa Theologica* in the thirteenth century, in which he differentiated sins by categories still used today. The *Summa* is hard reading for anyone but the most committed of theologians, but Aquinas's categorizations of sin helped give the church language for it.

- Consequently it is a mortal sin generically, whether it be contrary to the love of God, e.g. blasphemy, perjury, and the like, or against the love of one's neighbour, e.g. murder, adultery, and such like [. . .]. Sometimes, however, the sinner's will is directed to a thing containing a certain inordinateness, but which is not contrary to the love of God and one's neighbour, e.g. an idle word, excessive laughter, and so forth: and such sins are venial by reason of their genus.

Augustine lived and felt sin, but Aquinas intellectualized it, and the *Summa* is still taught to this day in seminaries and theology courses. It still forms the thinking of clergy. In Aquinas's thought, sin is essentially anything that involves a person turning away from God, but to differing degrees. The desire for goods, attention, the gratification of lust, and all manner of self-satisfying acts are, for Aquinas, occasions of sin. Venial sins can add up unless confessed, and mortal sins are ultimately destructive to a person's relationship with God, leading the way to apostasy.

Not everyone needs to or should make their way through the thickets of Aquinas's work. It was this kind of obsessive categorizing of sin and the eventual and probably inevitable selling of "indulgences" to buy off a sinner's time in purgatory that led Martin Luther to publish his Ninety-Five Theses, so in many ways, we can and should point to sin as the cause of the Reformation. But as a framework for understanding forgiveness, the Catholic understanding and codification of sin is crucial to understanding how forgiveness can be used to manipulate and abuse. Before the Reformation, Catholicism ruled most of the Western world, and these early Catholic teachings about sin became inextricably tied into law and government. Without this notion of sin, we don't have the Crusades; the Inquisition; confessionals being used as cover for emotional, sexual, and spiritual abuse; and much more. Catholic notions of sin, even stripped of the popery Martin Luther hated enough to cause him to start the Reformation, were so much a part of Western Christianity that they even influenced the Protestant-led Salem Witch Trials. And without sin, nobody would need forgiveness.

***

Donnie Johnson was a model inmate. A prison convert to Seventh Day Adventism, he was pious, prayerful, and became an elder in the church while serving a long sentence. On the day of his execution, he entered the lethal injection chamber singing hymns, and he prayed aloud for forgiveness for himself and for the executioners who killed him. And thirty-five years before Johnson chose death by lethal injection over the electric chair, he stuffed a garbage bag down his wife's throat, suffocating her, and then dumped her body in a shopping mall parking lot.

His son saw his father's prison turn to Christianity as a scam, saying of Johnson that "he's an evil human being" who can only "talk Christianity." His stepdaughter was more generous, telling lawyers she'd forgiven Johnson and that his death "will not feel like justice to me" because due to her stepbrother's estrangement, Johnson's death meant she would also lose the last connection to her mother. Johnson wrote in a statement requesting a stay of execution that he was "humbly" asking for forgiveness. "It is because of the person that I had became [sic]," Johnson wrote, "that I found I was not a man but a monster." But Johnson was confident that "the Lord in his mercy has forgiven me," and he told his family and his executioners he prayed they would forgive him too. As the drugs that would kill him were pumped into his arm, Johnson prayed aloud. "Into your hands, I commend my spirit."

Because Donnie Johnson is dead, we will never know which of his children was correct about the sincerity of his religious conversion. But we do know that Johnson, like so many other prisoners, pleaded for forgiveness and used a Christian framework for doing so. But what Johnson did to his wife was indeed monstrous and sinful. To take someone's life so violently, to admit to doing it without any seeming remorse, and to destroy his family is an unimaginable series of acts for most of us. And to convert while in prison, to repent, and to be forgiven by at least one of his children is the kind of detail any preacher would love to shoehorn into a Sunday sermon.

The death penalty is the ultimate punishment, one so abhorrent many countries don't even practice it. For a prisoner to spend the rest of their natural life in jail, cut off from the world and isolated from loved ones, seems in many cases to be punishment enough and has led to many cases of repentance and forgiveness as prisoners spend years mulling over their crimes. Restorative justice and prison abolition movements go even further, encouraging criminals to speak to the families of victims, work on atonement, and bring the community into the process rather than over-relying on often biased courts. In this scenario, for a person to be forgiven by their community or the families of victims, it's more than a one-on-one conversation between a person and God. In Donnie Jonson's case, the death penalty robs both the perpetrator and victims of any chance at a restorative justice process and the longer, harder, less superficial path to forgiveness. Restorative justice is an ongoing process of repentance, action, and change. It also requires an unlearning of what most of us were taught about sin and forgiveness. And much of that is rooted in misunderstandings of the Bible, the text that was at the center of the Salem Witch Trials, the founders' ideas of moral and ethical good, and most of our own contemporary understandings of forgiveness.

Before his public disgrace for abusing hundreds of girls in his years as a doctor for gymnasts, Larry Nassar was a model Catholic.

A weekly Mass goer, catechist, and church volunteer, he was the kind of person the media would describe as "devout." Rachel Denhollander, the first of Nassar's victims to speak up about her abuse, was also a victim of abuse at her Evangelical church as a child. In the *Washington Post*, she wrote that "misguided theology and a refusal to interact with experts on this issue led the church to miss—and then cover up—sexual abuse within its own walls."

Should Larry Nassar be forgiven? Should people who colluded in abuse like those who covered for Nassar be forgiven too? At the height of the Boston scandal, Cardinal Law, who covered up hundreds of cases of child abuse, begged forgiveness from those "who have suffered from my shortcomings and my mistakes." Law's funeral, held in the Vatican, contained no mention of this part of his life, which is his primary legacy. The presiding cardinal, Angelo Sondano, mentioned only that "each of us can sometimes be lacking in our mission." Pope Francis, to the chagrin of many, delivered the benediction over Law's coffin. The church may not have forgiven Law, but when he died, it looked the other way, yet again.

The Catholic Church wears a Janus face when it comes to forgiveness. It looks to a future where, ideally, abuse has ended and there is nothing to forgive. But it also looks to a past where protecting the institution, its finances, and its leadership led to years of silencing, which damaged victims even further. This same Janus face has revealed itself in entertainment, politics, sports, universities, and workplaces as the sins of harassment and abuse continue to be aired. On the one side, we see a future where abuse and harassment might happen less often thanks to those who have come forward. On the other, we see millennia of silencing, skepticism, and doubt.

In years of writing about these topics, I have found surprisingly little written in Catholic theology about sexual harassment, abuse, or forgiveness. Even after Boston, even after the Magdalene Laundries, even after the recent revelations of Catholic residential schools in Canada burying the bodies of hundreds of children, not much has been written about what forgiving abusers might mean. Much more has been written about this by female Protestant theologians, and particularly by female Protestant ethicists from denominations where women have been ordained for some time.

Perhaps having women in leadership positions means that this reckoning with abuse and forgiveness can be more of an open conversation. Perhaps, too, those women, many from the first generations to be ordained, had to deal with harassment and systemic misogyny themselves. Perhaps women in their congregations who'd been uncomfortable talking to male pastors about domestic and sexual violence were finally able to open up to these female religious leaders. And perhaps it's just how pervasive this problem is across every religious denomination, in every part of the country, and in nearly every workplace. Many women who have been harassed have described their emotional state as angry or humiliated. These are not emotional states that easily lead to forgiveness.

In an essay entitled "Love Your Enemy: Sex, Power and Christian Ethics," UCC pastor and professor Karen Lebaqz writes that the problem of expecting forgiveness is that it fails to understand that abused women "need to operate out of a 'hermeneutic of suspicion.'" In this mindset, forgiveness can appear to "ignore the role-conditioning or status of men and women in this culture." Lebaqz writes that forgiveness means "loving your enemy," thus asking us to redefine forgiveness, not as an act of losing "the self or the self's perspective, for this contradicts the value of survival." Another part of the problem is that we conceive forgiveness as a kind of sentimentality when in fact it is an issue of justice, both in recognizing injustice and in redressing it.

For Serene Jones, the president of Union Theological Seminary, the problem of forgiveness is tied up in the notion of universal sin, which she wrote about in *Sojourners* in February of 2018. In the Christian tradition, Jones writes, sin and sinfulness "pervades all of life." In terms of sexual violence, this universal sin "names how some are guilty of perpetrating grave harms, while others bear the direct effects of this sin on their victimized, traumatized bodies and minds." For Jones, the challenge for Christians is both admitting that the "war against women is real, ongoing, and church-sanctioned" and understanding that God "rejects this violence as sin and evil and stands beside all those who suffer from it and who fight against it."

In 1976, Marie Fortune founded the Faith Trust Institute, which works to help religious leaders address issues of sexual and domestic violence. The institute is still in operation today, working with interfaith clergy and laypeople. In an essay entitled "Preaching Forgiveness?" Fortune frames the issue by first defining what forgiveness is *not*. According to her, forgiveness is not "condoning or pardoning harmful behavior, which is a sin," or "healing the wound lightly." Forgiveness is not "always possible" and not "an expectation of any degree of future relationship with the person who caused the harm."

One Catholic theologian who has written on forgiveness and the sexual abuse of women is M. Shawn Copeland of Boston College. In her book *Enfleshing Freedom*, Copeland discusses forgiveness through the lens of slavery, which "rendered Black women's bodies objects of property, of production, of reproduction, of sexual violence." These women could not forgive their enslavers because "a human subject cannot consent to any treatment or condition that is intended to usurp the transcendental end or purpose for which human beings are divinely created."

That higher authority who leads to the transcendental end Copeland is describing might be God, but it might also be a slow, gradual shift in the structure of institutions that have smothered the voices of victims. And part of that shift might mean helping men, for example, to understand that their requests for forgiveness are a part of their patriarchal privilege. Those who have harassed and abused are absolved, and they move on. Sometimes they even move on into positions of great power, as Cardinal Law's move to Rome after Boston and the election of Donald Trump demonstrated.

The work of Sister Helen Prejean gives us another model for talking about forgiveness. Her decades of work to end the death penalty in America might make one assume she believes death row inmates should all be forgiven. But this is not the case. Rather, when Prejean describes looking into the eyes of killers and seeing their humanity, she is bringing them to a kind of reconciliation with themselves, with the "transcendental end for which human beings are created," as Copeland writes. Victims do not have to forgive those who rape, abuse, and harass us, because in those acts, in their reduction of our humanity, they deny us a fully lived life.

∗

This isn't a book specifically about the Bible, so I don't need to stop here and explain how it was written or how it has been historically abused. I will, however, step in for a moment to clarify a few things about my own understanding of the Bible. Primarily, I don't read Hebrew and only took one year of undergraduate Greek, so when it comes to understanding the intricacies and abuses of biblical language about forgiveness, experts are important. Secondly, this book is not based on a fundamentalist understanding of Scripture. In my understanding, God didn't write the Bible; we are only reading the words of Jesus second-, third-, or fourth-hand, and we must read the Bible in the cultural and religious context of the time it was written. Otherwise, we are only projecting our own biases and desires onto Scripture, including our own desires for forgiveness.

It is true that Jesus talks extensively about forgiveness in the Bible, but in Koine Greek, the language of the first written versions of the Gospels, he doesn't actually use any word that translates closely to our modern understanding of forgiveness. While the Old English *forgiefan* means something close to pardoning an offense or remitting debt, Merriam Webster's modern definition of *forgiveness* is "to cease to feel resentment against" someone or something.

But the Koine Greek word we translate today as "forgiveness" is *aphiēmi*. Rather than meaning something like the end of resentment, *aphiēmi* is closer to putting actual, physical distance between yourself and the person who's done you harm. In Matthew's version of the Lord's Prayer, the Greek version reads "*kai aphiēmi hemin hēmōn opheilēma*," which roughly means "put distance between us and our debts." The Greek scribes who may have talked to people who knew and followed Jesus would have understood his commandments to "forgive" in this way.

Jesus's own understanding of what forgiveness means would not be very close to our contemporary understanding either unless we happen to be Jewish. "סלח," which is sometimes translated as "forgive," or *salakh*, is often used in the Psalms and throughout the Hebrew scriptures. It's also heard in the liturgy for Yom Kippur. In a lexicon, *salakh* can sometimes mean "covering or atoning for sin, removing it, letting it pass, wiping it out, washing it away, cleansing it, and forgetting it." YHWH will "remove sin (Psalm 103:12) throwing it behind his back (Isaiah 38:17) or into the depths of the sea (Micah 7:19)." So Jesus, sitting in the temple, would have heard forgiveness described as an external action that God performs on behalf of people.

Salakh was a gift offered to a person who had already atoned for their sins, a pardon given by YHWH. In Psalm 131, David sings of forgiveness as redemption and deliverance.

Who pardons [ha-soleakh] all your iniquities, who heals all your diseases; who redeems your life from the pit, who crowns you with lovingkindness and compassion; who satisfies your years with good things, so that your youth is renewed like the eagle?

Throughout the Hebrew scriptures, however, the people keep distancing themselves from YHWH, which is why they continuously atone and seek forgiveness. The fact that Jewish people today continue to honor Yom Kippur, the holiest day of the Jewish year, as a time to fast and make amends demonstrates that this notion is so important that Jesus would also have heard this same emphasis on humility and atonement being necessary for forgiveness. The ashes many Christians put on their foreheads once a year to mark the beginning of the penitential season of Lent are a faint echo of the sackcloth and ashes Hebrew penitents had to wear as an external punishment marking them as sinners. Jesus knew that forgiveness had to cost us something and that it came not from human authorities but from God.

In her book *On Repentance and Repair*, Rabbi Danya Ruttenberg writes that there are two different Hebrew words used in the context of forgiveness. One is *mechila*, which she writes "might be better translated as 'pardon'" and has the connotation of "relinquishing a claim against an offender." The other word used to convey forgiveness is *Slicha,* which Rabbi Ruttenberg says includes the idea of looking "with a compassionate eye at the perpetrator" and having some empathy toward them, but only after they have begun the work of repentance.

But, according to Rabbi Ruttenberg, neither of these words denotes a restoration of any relationship between the wrongdoer and the victim. *Mechila* implies that "the chapter is closed," but it does not imply that the harm never happened or that there is an implied promise of a continuing relationship. *Slicha* does not include a requirement "that the victim act like nothing happened." The primary question that Jewish literature of repentance asks is not how a harm doer can move on but instead asks, "what needs to be done to close accounts?"

Dr. Thomas Bolin, a scholar of the Hebrew Bible, says that "morality and repentance in the Hebrew Bible is less interior and more that you have a miasma about you." Fasting, prayer, and confessions of sin depicted in the Hebrew Bible are external expressions, not internal ones. Biblical scholar David Lambert also describes the word *shuv,* used to describe returning to God, being used more to describe returning to the Jewish covenant with God rather than discovering the kind of internalized individual moral agency we might today understand as a prerequisite for forgiveness. The change Jesus understood people needed to make was external and thus tied to the idea that forgiveness is often about putting time and distance between yourself and the person who's harmed you. It was also about bringing a person back into the tribe, which helps us understand the parable of the prodigal son much more clearly. The son is forgiven not so that the father will feel better but so that the tribe will be healed by coming back together again.

"Forgiveness and anger are relational, and cultural circum-stances impact this," Dr. Bolin says. In Jesus's understanding, "being told to forgive does acknowledge you have a reason to be angry," but letting go of that anger is a form of nonretaliation, a radical choice in Jesus's time, when retaliation was thought to be a person's right. The Lord's Prayer, so central to Christian worship around the world, also emphasizes that forgiveness is more about God changing a person's desire to fight back and using that choice to not retaliate to change the society around us.

In the series of petitions that make up the prayer in Matthew's version, the most commonly used one, the penitent asks God for forgiveness, not other people: forgive *us* our debts, forgive *us* our sins, forgive *us* our trespasses. This is repeated for emphasis. In the Lord's Prayer, it is only once God has granted us forgiveness that we can grant the same thing to others.

But Jesus was not thinking of sending someone a Hallmark card to say sorry; in his Jewish understanding, we had to atone first, and forgiveness could mean sending someone away, putting distance between ourselves and someone who's harmed us, or even deciding never to see that person again. The simplistic definition of forgiveness as an end of resentment doesn't work for Jesus, and it should not necessarily work for us either. It is for these reasons that Judas is such a figure of fascination. In Matthew's Gospel, we're told Judas tried to give back the silver he received for betraying Jesus and later hanged himself. The early church fathers had a grand time imagining all kinds of gruesome deaths for Judas, including Papias of Hierapolis's notion that Judas somehow became so bloated by sin he couldn't pass through any doors, and that he somehow poured his innards into the land, which afterward stank for centuries.

Entertaining as these kinds of accounts might be, they don't answer the question of why Judas did not just ask Jesus for forgiveness. As the Son of God, Jesus would have been able to pardon Judas's sins, but Jesus seems instead to have chosen *aphiēmi* and to have sent Judas away. When preachers tell us that Jesus forgives everyone; that he always forgives; and that following in his model, we should do the same, that doesn't explain the disappearance of Judas. When Jesus is on the cross and "forgives" the people who kill him, he specifically does so because "they know *not* what they do," but Judas, like abusers and betrayers throughout history, knew exactly what he was doing. When Jesus "gives up his spirit" on the cross, the verb used is *salakh* again. Jesus releases debts owed him by his killers or those who failed to save him, like Judas and Peter. But because neither Judas nor Jesus's Roman killers repent, he actually can't forgive them. When he says, "father forgive them," he's making clear that only God can do that. It might not be a sentimental picture of forgiveness, but it's the one he left us with.

Another prominent occasion in the Gospels where Jesus's understanding of forgiveness has been garbled is in the story of the woman caught in adultery from the Gospel of John. I have heard this described many times as the story of Jesus forgiving a "sinful" or "fallen" woman. But it's a more subtle and complex story. In the Jewish understanding of *salakh*, the woman would have to repent in order to be forgiven, which she doesn't do. She stands silently as the Pharisees bring her before Jesus and grill him about whether she should be stoned according to the law of Moses. But Jesus doesn't wave them off, telling them she's forgiven, go in peace. Instead, he stays silent, writing on the ground (what, we'll never know, much to our frustration), until they ask him again, at which point he says,

"Let anyone among you who is without sin be the first to throw a stone at her." Of course, none of the Pharisees realize they're sinless, so they wander off, probably looking for another woman to throw stones at.

But in order to achieve the *teshuvah*, or repentance required for forgiveness, the woman would have to go to the person she's wronged; perform an act of appeasement, the equivalent of paying off a debt; and only then can she ask that specific person for forgiveness. We can assume that was her husband, but it wasn't Jesus. So he can't actually forgive her. What he can do instead is refuse to condemn her, and offer her some advice.

Jesus was left alone with the woman standing before him. Jesus straightened up and said to her, "Woman, where are they? Has no one condemned you?" She said, "No one, sir." And Jesus said, "Neither do I condemn you. Go your way, and from now on do not sin again."

"Do not sin again" could, of course, be interpreted as forgiveness. But biblical interpretation is always political and cultural. In a patriarchal society, the woman needs to be forgiven because she's indulged her sexual desire. But maybe she was forced into marriage with a much older man or an abusive man and has never known a tender or affectionate touch. Maybe her husband was also adulterous, a hardly uncommon thing in Jesus's time or our own, but her husband's not the one who's about to have stones thrown at him. Jesus doesn't ask about any of this. He just asks if anyone has condemned her and says he won't either. When he tells her not to sin again, that could be a warning not to get in the way of the Pharisees and their judgment more than any kind of moral condemnation. It could be a message to stay out of danger, much as we warn girls today not to walk alone at night. Or it could just be a friendly way of saying "stay out of trouble because I don't want you to die by stoning." What it means depends on the person interpreting it. But at no point does Jesus say to this woman, "I forgive you."

My friend Sophia's growing understanding of *aphiēmi* came during the pandemic. For over a decade, she had been part of a group of women that gathered monthly to pray, talk, and take care of one another. A few years before COVID-19 struck, one of the women in the group developed stage 4 cancer. The three women who stayed healthy cared for the woman with cancer until her death and talked about how they might continue to gather as a group by bringing in some new people. Then the pandemic prevented them from meeting in person, so they moved over to Zoom like everyone else, dealing with technical glitches and the frustrations of mute buttons and background noise.

But they were still taking care of one another and gathering, until one day one of the three remaining women from the first group sent an email saying she was done and joining another prayer group, with no explanation offered. This was during the most isolated months when there was no church, no gathering with family, and people were feeling lonely to extremes. Sophia was furious in a way she hadn't been since a friend had ditched her for a cooler group of kids in high school. It seemed that ten years of friendship, tending the sick, and caring for community were just gone, with no reason given.

Or so she thought. In the months to come, she'd occasionally get emails from the friend who'd dumped her, chatty and friendly messages asking how she was doing and seeing if she wanted to get coffee. Sophia didn't reply. It was clear that her friend wanted to be forgiven. But Sophia just didn't know how to respond.

Nearly a year and a half went by before she finally got a message from her former friend about another mutual friend who had also died suddenly. As she read it, her thoughts weren't about anger or a need for distance but about the person who had died. The fact that the former friend took the time to tell her felt like the permission she needed to understand that this was *teshuvah*, the gift of hearing it from someone who knew the departed person instead of hearing it from a stranger, and Sophia could finally release some of the anger she'd been holding for so long. It didn't erase things or repair them entirely, but it allowed her to say, "Thank you for telling me." Without *aphiēmi*, however, it wouldn't have happened. Time and distance were necessary.

In *No Future without Forgiveness*, his book about the South African Truth and Reconciliation Commission, the late archbishop Desmond Tutu writes that South African Christians were able to do the work of repentance and repair after apartheid because of the Ngumi Bantu word *ubuntu*, meaning humanity, which is also used in the Xhosa language to also mean a kind of universal bond and sense of shared responsibility. *Ubuntu*, Tutu writes, means my humanity is caught up, inextricably bound up, in theirs. We belong in a bundle of life. We say "a person is a person through other people." It is not "I think therefore I am." It says rather "I am human because I belong." I participate, I share. A person with *ubuntu* is open and available to others, affirming to others, does not feel threatened that others are able and good; for he or she has a proper self-assurance that comes from knowing that he or she belongs in a greater whole and is diminished when others are humiliated or diminished, when others are tortured or oppressed, or treated as if they were less than who they are.

Without *ubuntu*, Tutu says that there is no way that Black South Africans would have been able to move past decades of oppression at the hands of white colonizers. It was *ubuntu* and care for his community that sustained Nelson Mandela through his years in prison and guided Tutu in the work of the Truth and Reconciliation Commission after apartheid came to an end. Because the work of the commission was broadcast globally and shared in news around the world, it was also for many people their first encounter with the concept of restorative justice, which makes the work of repentance and repair collective and community-focused, in contrast to Americans' individualistic understandings of forgiveness.

In many ways, Jesus's understandings of forgiveness were closer to Tutu's definition of *ubuntu* than they were to a simplistic notion that we forgive to allow the person who did wrong to "move on." This notion of collective participation in the process also means that the victim doesn't feel the lifting of a burden so much as a sense that they can now rejoin the community. Reparations can lead to repair, and repair is what brings us back together again, in many ways more than forgiveness. Of course, in the centuries since Jesus offered us these examples, they have been twisted and distorted in every manner possible. But that doesn't mean we can't go back to the beginning and forgive ourselves for getting them so wrong.

3

Forgiveness, American Style

Unlike thousands of other Americans who were obsessed with it, I didn't see the musical *Hamilton* until recently. Of course, I knew about it—for a time, you couldn't avoid *Hamilton* quotes and gifs on social media or overhear awkwardly rapped versions of its songs heard in snatches from passing cars. But during the pandemic, to fill in the gaps in my knowledge of American history during what felt like a historical pivot point, I read Ron Chernow's massive Hamilton biography, which had inspired Lin-Manuel Miranda to write the musical.

By the time I managed to score a half-price ticket in the highest nosebleed seats to the live show of *Hamilton* in San Francisco, however, the musical had gone from critically beloved to the subject of cultural backlash. Miranda's choice to portray the founders as people of color wasn't the problem; his choice to nearly avoid the subject of slavery altogether in the musical was. The Black writer Ishmael Reed went so far as to write a Christmas Carol–style play called *The Haunting of Lin-Manuel Miranda*, where the playwright is visited by ghosts of dead slaves, Native Americans, poorly treated women, and many others who eviscerate the play's half-truths and "corny" rhymes. For some audiences, *Hamilton* represents a larger American propensity to dismissively wave away American historical sins. *Hamilton* also reflects a theological tendency throughout American history that believes wrongs are easily erased and the wrongdoer only needs to feel bad for a brief amount of time.

What happens in the play to Hamilton's wife Eliza exemplifies this. Hamilton, who Chernow says had "worked to achieve a spotless reputation as treasury secretary" and who Miranda treats with admiration bordering on the hagiographic, starts repeatedly cheating on his long-suffering wife about midway through the play, and audiences are rapidly asked to believe that this is alright.

When the husband of Maria Reynolds, the woman Hamilton was sleeping with, began asking Hamilton for hush money, Hamilton paid up and just kept on sleeping with Maria and paying her husband's bribes. This effectively forced Maria into a kind of prostitution. In the musical and in history, when this becomes a public scandal, Hamilton both eviscerates and defends himself in "The Reynolds Pamphlet," calling the experience a "mortifying disappointment." In the musical, this leads to Hamilton's wife Eliza singing a big Broadway-style ballad about burning his letters and "erasing herself from the narrative." The audience at the live show ate this scene up, watching a woman getting her revenge on her cheating husband with actual fire.

But while I was irritated by the musical's many historical distortions, I didn't really get upset until a couple of scenes later, when the Hamiltons' son Phillip dies in a duel, leading to a scene of Phillip's parents standing by his graveside. At this point, Miranda depicts them holding hands and has the chorus burst into a round of "Forgiveness, can you imagine?" For emphasis, the chorus repeats this same line several times.

Just like that, when their son has died because of his father's terrible advice about dueling and her husband has publicly and privately humiliated her on multiple occasions, Eliza Hamilton—who seems by all accounts to have been nobody's fool—suddenly loses all of her deserved rage at her husband and turns into the perfect picture of Christian forgiveness, spending the rest of her life devoted to restoring the public image of her husband after his own death in a duel. Yes, the real Eliza was a deeply religious person, but this sentimentalized notion that forgiveness is just that easy and accompanied by a soaring chorus of praise had me squirming in my seat and muttering, "Bullshit."

Of course, some of the problem with this depiction of a wife who has been humiliated and cheated on being so forgiving is that, as with so many women throughout history, we don't know how Eliza really felt. Her decision to burn some of their correspondence is part of this, but she lived nearly fifty years longer than her husband and seems to have made a choice to stay quiet on the issue. While she did go on to dedicate much of her life to preserving the better parts of her husband's legacy, there is not much historical evidence that she wrote or spoke about his affair outside of the privacy of her family and friends. Her story is a reminder that the narrative of forgiveness is often told by the person who has been forgiven and not by the person granting forgiveness. The musical probably wouldn't have racked up over a billion dollars in ticket sales if Eliza had done what many women would choose today, and hired a good divorce lawyer to take Hamilton for all he was worth.

Everyone who does wrong wants to be forgiven, and this is why we are captivated by narratives of forgiveness. From the days when the Bible was first written to today, the story of forgiveness is often as oversimplified as the story of Eliza forgiving Alexander. But forgiveness isn't linear, and it isn't necessarily something that happens in a moment. Sometimes it can take decades, or hundreds, if not thousands, of years. Sometimes a person stands in for an institution when it comes to forgiveness, an imperfect solution in cases like popes having to beg for forgiveness on behalf of the entire history of missionary Catholicism or presidents asking Americans to forgive the country its history of war, genocide, and slavery. But these stories of repentance immediately bringing about forgiveness being repeated over and over again means that these simplistic notions of forgiveness continue to be held up as exemplary today, and they are very much part of the American imagination.

Like his fellow founder Thomas Jefferson, who was perfectly happy to take a razor to the Bible and eliminate passages about anything miraculous, Hamilton's attitude toward religion was idiosyncratic. His chagrin about the Reynolds affair comes off as more defensive than penitential as he repeatedly points the finger at

Reynolds's husband as the cause of the affair rather than taking the blame for it himself. Having been born out of wedlock, as a child, Hamilton watched as his mother was denied Christian burial, and his own relationship with religion became more private than public. As an adult, he almost never attended church, although his family rented a pew at Trinity Episcopal Church in New York, but he was also reported to pray frequently on his own. Hamilton's vision of America was of a religious free market, a place where "a perfect equality of religious privileges" was available to anyone.

Hamilton and Jefferson's idea of America as the land of religious reinvention is one of the many significant outcomes of the Reformation. Forgiveness itself didn't cause the Reformation, but abuse of Christ's messages about forgiveness played a huge part in the fracturing of the early church and the repercussions of that, which play out even today. The Reformation also raised questions about where forgiveness comes from (either from other people or from God) that we also still argue about to this day. It has led Americans to a kind of secularized theology of forgiveness, one in which forgiveness can lead to an erasure of history for the sake of the person or the country that feels a need to move on. That in turn can lead to persistent and pervasive forms of abuse, and it has repeatedly contributed to some of the more xenophobic and racist chapters in American history.

***

Indulgences evolved during the Middle Ages as a system by which penitential Catholics could pay money to the church to lessen their time in purgatory. While indulgences may have begun as a means to spur the faithful to greater acts of charity, the massive gaps between rich and poor in the Middle Ages meant impoverished, pious peasants pinched pennies to be forgiven of their sins. Meanwhile, they lived through waves of plagues, watching their loved ones drop dead left and right, and hoped to avoid a torturous afterlife. And the church being run by fallible and greedy human beings meant that this practice of taking money for indulgences was inevitably going to be abused. The young German monk Martin Luther was particularly infuriated by a Dominican papal agent named Johannes Tetzel, who is credited with the phrase "When the coin in the coffer rings / the soul from purgatory springs."

In Luther's Ninety-Five Theses, indulgences are a primary source of his reformative overtones. In the eighty-sixth thesis, Luther writes, "Why does not the pope, whose wealth today is greater than the wealth of the richest Crassus, build the basilica of St. Peter with his own money rather than with the money of poor believers?" At this juncture, Luther was still working out his doctrine of salvation and formulating his theory that human salvation does not depend on both good works and grace but on God's grace alone. Luther went so far as to send a copy of the Theses to the Vatican in protest of indulgences, but it would take decades more before the Catholic Church stopped charging for them.

While the Catholic Church no longer charges for them, indulgences, in fact, still exist today. When I was in Rome in 2016 during the papal Year of Mercy, a jubilee declared by Pope Francis, church doors all over the world and especially in Rome were declared to be "holy doors" and supposed to be left open. By passing through these and praying for forgiveness, a person could earn an indulgence. On a particularly hot and humid September day in St. Peter's square, I saw groups of pilgrims forming, following a set of prayers on a card handed to them by volunteers and moving slowly toward the massive basilica doors.

Jet lagged and confused, I shuffled my way into a group of Eastern European pilgrims and started following the set of prayers, but the heat got the best of me and I began to wander off in search of shade. So when an Italian cop waved me toward the doors, without thinking, I skipped the lines and entered the basilica through the designated holy doors. Therefore, I accidentally earned a plenary indulgence, which technically wiped away every sin I'd ever committed—let's be honest, an exhaustively long list—and this meant that if I had immediately dropped dead from the Roman heat wave, I would have gone straight to heaven. Unfortunately, I got gelato instead, and given the fact that gluttony is a sin and I got three scoops, like almost everyone else who gets an indulgence, I just went straight back to sinning.

When Luther began to formulate his critiques of indulgences, discontent with the practice spread quickly among frustrated Catholics who were tired of paying a fee for their salvation. As Luther's ideas began to migrate across Europe, they eventually led not only to Luther's own excommunication for heresy but to the reinvention of Christian ideas of forgiveness from something that could be earned by works to something earned by faith alone. Perhaps the greatest influence on this thinking today comes from John

Calvin, the Reformer who wrote of Catholic ideas of forgiveness being earned through both confession and good works that "they are wonderfully silent concerning the inward renewal of the mind, which bears with it true correction of life."

For Calvin and other Reformers, outward acts of confession and works did little to change the inward disposition toward sin. To be forgiven, rather than focusing on how our sins might impact others, we need to "fix our eyes upon the Lord's mercy alone." Calvin also thought that confession between believers to "lay our infirmities on one another's breasts" was enough and that confession to priests was unnecessary. But while this concept might seem empowering, the early Reformers were so focused on God that the writer and philosopher Voltaire wrote that they "turned all society into a convent," banished music and theater, and turned Geneva into a dour shadow of its former self. According to Voltaire, Reformers "condemned auricular confession, but they enjoined a public one," and as a result, penance, which had once been between the priest and the penitent, became performative, something that would play out in the early years of the American colonies as well and go on to have aftereffects in the American justice system.

Calvin's belief in unconditional election, the idea that some people are predestined to salvation and others are not, still has echoes in many forms of Christianity today. When it comes to notions of forgiveness, however, the Anglican church, which also arose from the Reformation and arguably shaped much of the American founders' anxiety about avoiding a state religion, still held to the idea that priests were there to help penitents confess sins and be forgiven. Henry VIII, who was raised as a Catholic and once received a plenary indulgence himself for traveling to a holy site, later upended the church so he could divorce his first wife, and in doing so, empowered his advisor Thomas Cromwell to rid England of "superstitions" like pilgrimages. Cromwell also closed England's monasteries and convents, and those who refused to leave them were publicly hanged. Henry, however, waffled on the issue of confession. He rejected Luther's notion of faith alone and deemed auricular confession necessary but continued in his own private devotions, which may have even included confessing to his own spiritual advisors.

Today, most people who belong to denominations that arose from the Reformation, like Lutherans, Methodists, and Presbyterians, don't practice private confession. However, the Anglican communion does, although it doesn't require it or see it as sacramental like the Catholic Church. Fr. Cody Maynus, an Episcopal priest, told me that confession in the Anglican communion is "a conversation between the penitent, God, and the church." Instead of the Catholic notion that a priest is a literal vessel for God's power to forgive, the Anglican communion instead sees confession as a form of "pastoral care," a chance for a priest to "give voice" to God's forgiveness.

With Anglican confession's roots in Catholic doctrine, however, the Puritans who arrived in America were fleeing liturgical practices just like it. Puritanism in England was a rejection of ritual and an embrace of Calvinist notions of sin and predestination. Puritans brought to America the idea of covenant theology, which taught that God's covenant with Adam and Eve demanded spiritual perfection, believed to have been fulfilled in the blameless life and sacrificial death of Jesus. Puritans today are typically portrayed as dour, judgmental, and cruel, and that seems not to be far from the truth. They often utilized public punishments like stocks and pillories, which frightened many people away from bad behavior but also made it harder for Puritans to conceptualize a forgiving or merciful God. They also had a horror of Catholics, which contributed to the anti-Catholic attitudes of many Americans, which would linger for centuries, and which would foreshadow xenophobic fears of immigrants and their "anti-Christian" religious practices, even when some of those immigrants were in fact Christians.

In rejecting the control England and its king had over their lives, America's founders were also fleeing a religion led by a king or queen, and to this day, the King of England is still considered the head of the Anglican church. America's founders were suspicious of the idea of a state religion and put the idea into the first phrase of the first amendment of the Constitution, thus emphasizing how paramount this concept was to them. "Congress shall make no law respecting an establishment of religion, or prohibiting the free exercise thereof" is an idea that may have subsequently been used and abused by conservatives and liberals alike, but it remains essential to the American vision of self-creation. To kick off the shackles of British rule, Americans had to reinvent everything from the ground up: government, art, music, theater, literature, and, yes, God. And in reinventing God, they also reinvented forgiveness.

America was founded by Protestants, and that same Protestant idea that clergy cannot be the mediators of forgiveness has impacted how America treated non-Protestants for a very long time. Fear of Catholics in particular as agents of the pope is still so rooted in American history that it remains present in some American Protestant communities to this day. Puritan fears of "popery" and the Catholic Church as the "whore of Babylon" became entangled with racism, xenophobia, and ethnocentrism as the country and its prejudices grew.

Hostility against Irish Catholic immigrants was so widespread that in 1844, Massachusetts politician Joseph Brickingham wrote that Catholics had brought to America a "plentitude of generosity which has induced us to feed the hungry." To be clear, Brickingham thought this was a bad idea. The danger was that "Irishmen fresh from the bogs of Ireland are led up to vote like dumb brutes . . . to vote down intelligent, honest, native Americans." Perhaps obviously, he was not talking about Indigenous Americans here because by this time, their population was being decimated thanks to that same ethnocentric streak. He was talking instead about white Protestant men.

Even after they fought on the Union side in the Civil War and showed their loyalty to America, Irish, Italians, Poles, and other Catholic immigrants from Europe were still denied work and housing, treated with suspicion, and sometimes became the victims of mob violence. The Ku Klux Klan was so paranoid about Catholics taking over America that in 1921 they assassinated Fr. James Coyle, an Irish Catholic priest living in Alabama. By the time John

F. Kennedy became America's first Catholic president in 1960, this anti-Catholic sentiment still hadn't entirely faded away because Kennedy repeatedly had to remind people that he was not the Catholic candidate for president but "the Democratic party's candidate who happens to be a Catholic."

Kennedy wasn't exactly a perfect Catholic, as his history of affairs with dozens of women reveals, but his mother, Rose, did write to his wife, Jaqueline, and told her to "remind Jack of his Easter duty" and attend confession. But while his election did mark the beginning of the end of some of the more public anti-Catholic prejudices in American history, the suspicion itself reflects very different ideas about forgiveness that remain part of American Christian religious thinking today. And one unfortunate historical turn for formerly oppressed European Catholic immigrants was that many of them became virulently racist. In the case of Irish Catholics in particular, many of them went into careers in law enforcement, people who had been under the boot effectively becoming the bootheel.

It's overly simplistic to say that Protestants think forgiveness comes from God alone and Catholics think it requires God, good works, and sacramental forgiveness from a priest. But the truth is that Protestant emphasis on forgiveness without the mediation of clergy has meant that Americans see forgiveness as a more individualistic process than the idea in the Hebrew Bible that it is meant to bring a person back into a community.

The Church of Jesus Christ of Latter Day Saints, one of the first religions founded in America, also reflects this individualistic American notion of forgiveness. Joseph Smith was born in 1805, and as a child growing up in Western New York, he was exposed to the Second Great Awakening, a time of great religious fervor with emotive preaching and religious experimentation. Smith's vision of an angel who handed him plates engraved with the story of an ancient American civilization would become the Book of Mormon, and Smith's charisma and idiosyncratic twists on Christian faith rapidly attracted a large number of followers. The fact that Smith was assassinated for his beliefs likely added to the allure of Mormonism, since the Puritan flight from religious oppression is part of the myth of the foundation of American history.

The Book of Mormon seems to portray a God more like John Calvin's than one who promises universal salvation. In its Doctrine and Covenants, God says, "I, the Lord, will forgive whom I will forgive, but of you it is required to forgive all men." Joseph Smith also wrote that in order to receive the "divine manifestation" of his visions, he had to first pray to God for forgiveness. Latter Day Saints don't practice confession like Catholics do in the sacramental sense, but "confession is a necessary requirement for complete forgiveness," according to LDS Bishop Richard Clarke, and Latter Day Saints are encouraged to confess to the person they've wronged, to God, and sometimes to a local member of the LDS priesthood if their sins are sexual in nature. Latter Day Saints also require confession as part of the "worthiness interview" a convert must go through in order to join a temple, and children are expected to begin confessing and asking for forgiveness around the age of eight. LDS beliefs are complex, but their ideas about sexual purity, individual salvation, and a God who decides which people He will forgive and which He won't bear much in common with the Protestant traditions Joseph Smith grew up surrounded by.

As Evangelical churches grew in the twentieth century, so, too, did the idea that a personal relationship with Jesus was more important than a sense of responsibility to the community. Norman Vincent Peale, pastor to the family of Fred Trump, father of Donald Trump, wrote that resentment can make a person "physically ill," so they should forgive not for the sake of others but in order to avoid making themselves sick. Billy Graham, perhaps America's best-known Evangelical, once described forgiveness as something for the most "sin-laden, selfish, evil person" because "sin breaks our fellowship with God." Forgiveness was for the good of the person being forgiven, not the community they lived in. And this changed American politics as well.

As conservative Catholics and conservative Evangelicals became more tightly knit in the 1980s, these lines about individualism and forgiveness became even blurrier. Where in the past American Catholics had put care for the poor, the immigrant, and the stranger at the top of their priorities, Evangelical focus on abortion, sex, and the body that were direct hand-me-downs from the country's Puritan roots started to change the preaching of Catholic bishops, who became entangled in the fight against abortion. This in turn changed Catholic clergy. The same personal relationship with Jesus Christ that mattered so much to Evangelicals became important to Catholics as well, but it also cost the communities Catholics served as the bishops of the American Catholic Church became more judgmental and less forgiving.

Writing to the Jesuit priest and war resister Dan Berrigan in 1972, when he was serving a prison sentence for burning Vietnam draft cards with homemade napalm, Catholic Worker founder Dorothy Day, who had herself done plenty of time in prison, said that she appreciated the sacrament of confession because, unlike the court of law, "the verdict there is always 'not guilty.'" But in shifting their focus to issues of the body like abortion and the sexual lives of LGBTQ people, the American Catholic bishops, who still claim to practice celibacy, gradually began to sound more and more like everyone was guilty except for them. That they did so while revelations about sex abuse began to become public is not coincidental. The fact remains that while the Catholic sacrament of confession and absolution may be far from perfect and may have in its own way contributed to the church's issues of spiritual and physical abuse, the confessional itself remains a unique space for people to work out the issue of forgiveness far from the prying eyes of the public.

American history, on the other hand, has often made forgiveness performative. After the murder of George Floyd in 2020, it seemed for a moment that every product you purchased came with a side order of an apology to the Black community. In a country where corporations stand in for people, hearing that Ben and Jerry's thinks that Black Lives Matter probably didn't feel like repentance to George Floyd's children. A Black person I know told me he'd never had that many white people asking him for forgiveness than he did in the summer of 2020. But it didn't last long.

That same summer, Scott Hancock, a historian from Gettysburg College, wrote in the *Journal of the Civil War Era* that sincere apology from white people, "while important, is not sufficient." After the Civil War, Hancock writes, public apologies became commonplace, both because Christianity had a strong influence at the time and because the granting of forgiveness could be a form of protection for vulnerable, newly freed people. By forgiving their enslavers, formerly enslaved people could not be accused by whites of bitterness or spite and were therefore thought to be less likely to seek out revenge. Beneath this narrative, however, "African Americans also knew that apologies, repentance and forgiveness would never be enough to move white society to make substantive changes." According to Hancock, until America can honestly confront and deconstruct white supremacy, white Americans will continue to sporadically issue apologies without actually doing anything about racism, and Black Americans will continue to be forced to perform forgiveness, even when they don't sincerely feel it. If asking for forgiveness means making a commitment to change to better society for all its members, white Americans have consistently failed at this, and there is blood on the ground to prove it.

One story from history that has frequently been misrepresented and twisted around to suit the notion of forgiveness as personal rather than collective salvation is the meeting of Frederick Douglass and his former enslaver. Douglass, who escaped from the plantation of Thomas Auld in 1838, went on to become a well-known orator, author, abolitionist, and even an advisor to President Lincoln. By the time he went to visit Auld in 1877, Douglass was, by most American standards of the time, a famous and financially successful man with a stellar reputation among liberals. But the idea that this was a visit where a formerly enslaved person would forgive the man who had terrorized him and his family is a distortion of the historical record. In one article on the History Channel website, the phrase "they cried and reminisced" is used to describe their meeting, making it sound like a sentimental encounter between old friends. And a Christian blogger refers to Douglass's meeting with Auld on Auld's deathbed as an "affirmation" of Auld's humanity and a moment of repentance for racism.

This notion that Douglass forgave Auld is a manipulation of Douglass's own ideals. While Douglass was a devout Christian who believed in dialogue between people on both sides of the slavery debate and was often criticized for it, he never argued that this meant enslavers should be forgiven. He believed in a common sense of humanity, but he also understood that the American desire to wipe the slate clean was a deliberate erasure of the pain and suffering he himself had endured. "Well the nation may forget," he said in an 1888 speech, "but the colored people of this country are bound to keep the past in lively memory until justice shall be done them."

According to the historian Robert Levine, Douglass described Auld's chief characteristic as "intense selfishness," suggesting the idea that Douglass was in any way empathetic toward Auld was probably an exaggeration. In Douglass's own words:

[Auld] had struck down my personality, had subjected me to his will, made property of my body and soul, reduced me to a chattel, hired me out to a noted slave breaker to be worked like a beast and flogged into submission; he had taken my hard earnings, sent me to prison, offered me for sale, broken up my Sunday-school, forbidden me to teach my fellow slaves to read [. . .] and pocketed the price of my flesh.

Nonetheless, Douglass, who was an ordained minister in the African Methodist Episcopal Zion church, believed in the power of Christian witness. When Auld was eighty-one and in poor health, Auld, who had apparently been following Douglass's career and may have even read his books, invited Douglass to his home. Levine writes that while there was "something undeniably moving about the reunion scene itself," Douglass was also aware that the conversation was being listened in on and reported on. Douglass was at that point so well known that news of the visit had disseminated before it even took place.

With this idea of an audience and history in mind, Douglass went into the encounter in the role of an empathetic listener, holding his former enslaver's palsied hand and listening as Auld said Douglass had always been "too smart to be a slave." One can only imagine how Douglass, who had been prevented from teaching his fellow enslaved people to read by Auld, received this. But while the scene would be manipulated into a sentimentalized story of forgiveness, what was in fact happening, according to Levine and other historians, was not forgiveness at all. It was instead a moment of social reversal.

Douglass, the former enslaved people, was now stronger and more powerful than the man who had enslaved him and his family. Noelle Trent of the National Civil Rights Museum says that "any interpretation of this encounter that says Black people need to suck it up and forgive white people in order to have peace misses the mark completely." Trent adds that the meeting of Douglass and Auld "is not a lesson in forgiveness. This is a lesson in personal reconciliation." Ka'mal McClarin, a historian with the National Parks Service, adds that the meeting was really a "victory lap" for Douglass, who wanted to show Auld his success after escaping from enslavement.

Formerly enslaved people, in fact, never owed their enslavers or the nation any forgiveness because they were never offered any atonement. To this day, this is why conversations about reparations to Black Americans are necessary. If forgiveness really happens when a person is offered amends for their suffering, that has never happened for Black Americans, who still deal with generational trauma and racism that is built into the idea of America today. The founders who wrote the Constitution were themselves mostly enslavers, including Alexander Hamilton himself, who wrote against slavery with one hand while buying and selling human beings for his in-laws and possibly for himself with the other.

When Thomas Jefferson wrote the Declaration of Independence, he enslaved hundreds of people, more than one of whom he is likely to have raped. When Ona Judge escaped from George Washington's Mount Vernon, he described her as "unfaithful" and spent the rest of his life trying to recapture her. Do the descendants of the people Jefferson and Washington enslaved owe these men forgiveness? In exchange for the idea of a free nation and a democracy, America chose chattel slavery, humiliation, and pain. For many Americans, forgiveness is viewed as primarily individual, a sort of self-reinvention that does not need to include communal repair, which makes America unable to deal with its true historical sins. In an individualistic society founded by people who considered religion a path to personal rather than collective salvation, a person being forgiven means, in some way, that they have triumphed over their own sinfulness. But this does not negate collective historical pain or change the toxic patterns of glossing over historical trauma that have scarred American history. And until that pain has ended—and given racism's trenchant grip on the American imagination, it is hard to say when or if that will happen—no Black American or any of their descendants owe those men forgiveness. That doesn't make for a great Broadway song and dance number. But it is, at the very least, honest.

4

The Conquered Body

Trauma and the Burden of Forgiveness

By the time people at my workplace began appending land acknowledgments to their email signatures in recent years, the Ohlone people who had lived on the land the university was built on had been largely decimated and scattered for many decades. The emails may be sent from Ohlone land, but there are very few Ohlone left to claim it.

Land acknowledgments are a kind of apology, a gesture at asking for forgiveness, like sticking a Black Lives Matter sticker on your car or giving a bit of money to the United Farm Workers. But for white people, they are another gesture at trying to make amends for the sins of our ancestors. Whether your white ancestors arrived in America with the pilgrims or even as comparatively recently as most white Californians who began pouring into the state in the 1850s Gold Rush, you have still benefited from the conquering of lands that belonged to someone else. Native American activists have become increasingly vocal about this, and, increasingly, white Americans have tried to offer apologies. But do these gestures really mean that anyone is owed forgiveness? And can the genocide of Native American people, or any people conquered by others, ever truly be forgiven?

Because we have so long been conditioned to understand that forgiving also means forgetting, that way of thinking has been a means for abuse to be perpetuated both on mass scales like the Holocaust and in private. For people who have survived abuse and trauma, however, telling them to forget the source of their trauma can cause feelings of hopelessness, guilt, and shame, and can perpetuate cycles of abuse. And while white Americans may ask for forgiveness from the descendants of enslaved people and from Native American people, if we benefit from institutionalized racism in any way, are we really owed it?

A 2015 study by psychologists of the concept of forgive and forget found that most people forgive in two ways. Decisional forgiveness is a conscious decision to let go of hurt feelings and move forward, "free of the effects those feelings can bring." Emotional forgiveness involves replacing negative emotions toward someone who has wronged you with positive ones, like compassion or empathy. But while most psychologists argue forgiving can help a person move past trauma, another study in 2011 found that being forgiving can perpetuate and excuse abusive behavior in personal relationships. While many Christians would argue there is no such thing as being "too forgiving," the fact of the matter is that while forgiveness should theoretically prevent people from reoffending, in many cases, it actually gives them permission to do so.

As we also learn more about trauma theory and epigenetics, it becomes clear that even if a member of a historically oppressed group were to be exceptionally forgiving and try to move past the history of violence and abuse done to their ancestors, their bodies may tell a different story. While there are multiple sociological reasons that Black and Native American people have worse mortality outcomes than white people, epigenetics is also helping us to understand that trauma can alter your DNA. And the more we also understand the intrinsic connections between physical and mental health, the more we can also understand that conditions like anxiety, depression, and addiction can be passed down just like diabetes, high blood pressure, and heart disease. So, again, should the people whose ancestors' bodies and minds were so deeply violated that generations who have come after them are still suffering the effects of those violations be expected to forgive? And why would they ever be expected to forget?

For more than twenty years, I've taught at the University of California, Berkeley. Many of my classes meet in the Social Science building, known until 2021 as Barrows Hall. The man for whom Barrows Hall was named, David Prescott Barrows, was an anthropologist who wrote multiple racist screeds against Black and Filipino people. Berkeley's Building Name Review Committee voted to strip his name from the building that is ironically home to the Ethnic Studies department. Barrows and the others whose names are being removed are long dead, so it is impossible for them to ask for forgiveness. The university, state, or country, instead, must stand in for individuals.

Institutions are increasingly forced to ask for forgiveness on behalf of people both living and deceased. The process is frequently arduous and clunky, and the results are often unsatisfying for living victims or their descendants. But institutions rarely follow best practices when they are accused of abuse. When these reports surface, transparency and accountability are paramount. But an apology and promise to do better are not enough to earn an institution forgiveness. Still, people whose families were enslaved or abused are often expected to put that in the past.

And when an abusive person's name is drilled off a building, the shadow of the old name often remains visible, even when a new one is mounted on top of it, gouges in the surface that never fully fade away. When a statue of Christopher Columbus, a confederate general, or the missionary Junipero Serra is toppled in protest, the pedestal often remains. The same can be said about institutions with histories of abuse. Apologies may be offered, but the sordid history is now visible to everyone, hiding in plain sight. And abuse being visible to everyone does not mean it deserves to be forgiven. It just means we can theoretically see it more clearly when it inevitably happens again.

***

California's oldest standing buildings are mostly the missions, built by an ambitious Spanish Franciscan named Junipero Serra. Serra, who arrived in Baja California in the late 1760s, had a singular goal: to convert as many of the seemingly recalcitrant Native Californian people as possible. Considering how many Native people ran away from missionaries, they likely weren't so much recalcitrant as terrified. Some Native people once brought a sick baby to Serra, who assumed they wanted it baptized, and then fled when Serra appeared to be about to drown it.

As Serra slowly made his way up California, building missions as he went, more and more Native Californians were converted to Christianity, but once they converted, rather than finding salvation, their lives became desperate and miserable. Not allowed to leave the missions, they were often separated from family members; stripped of their languages, rituals, and cultures; and forced to labor for the church. Disease and hunger were rampant, and Native Californians were beaten, whipped, and treated with a condescending, infantilizing attitude by missionaries.

By the time I was born, California's population had been reshaped many times over. Oakland, where I grew up, had gone from a city of Italian and Irish immigrants to a city with a more than 50 percent Black population during the Great Migration. Immigrants from Mexico and Central America began to pour into California, alongside people from all over Asia, Southeast Asia, and Africa. But there were always Native Californians too. It's just that thanks to Serra, not many of them were left.

So, our teachers, with a mind toward building a story of California that made room for that multiplicity of narrators, took us on field trips to see the Miwok Village at Point Reyes National Seashore, alongside the tours of missions that are ritualistic for every California child. But in my generation, as Native Americans began to demand a reckoning for historical wrongs, instead of hearing stories praising Serra, we began to hear other stories: of disease and death, of cultures wiped out, of people who had once been rich in land now homeless. We learned this way that some things are unforgivable.

Among those stories, one has stuck with me for fifty years as an example of what it means to decimate a group of people so utterly that there is no possibility of forgiveness and defined both what it means to commit an unforgivable act and how that act can have repercussions for generations. On August 29, 1911, a starving Native man wandered into Oroville, California, where he was cornered by dogs. He was Yahi, a tribe that had been deliberately and violently massacred by white settlers to the area. In the 1840s, there were approximately four hundred Yahi living in Northern California. By 1911, there was one.

The town reached out to the University of California Museum of Anthropology, which was at that time located in San Francisco, seeking help for this man, whose name was unknown. Alfred Kroeber, who ran the museum, proposed that the man be moved into the museum rather than repatriated to a reservation in Oklahoma. Because it was a Yahi custom not to speak his name to outsiders, Kroeber began calling him Ishi, meaning "man." Ishi suffered from numerous health problems in the museum, where he lived for four and a half years. In one of the first photographs taken of Ishi, he is thin, covered in what looks like a loaned coat, and barefoot. The anthropologist James Clifford writes that this image, widely circulated when Ishi was "discovered," was the beginning of Ishi's story being stolen from him. "Stripped of any context, he is pure artifact, available for collection; pure victim, ready to be rescued."

Kroeber considered Ishi a friend, and he and other UC anthropologists tried to learn Ishi's language and customs, hoping to preserve them. But their methodology was, by today's standards, dehumanizing. Ishi was advertised as "the last wild Indian in California" and essentially put on display in the museum, where he would carve obsidian arrowheads and sing Yahi songs for crowds of tourists. Against his will, Ishi traveled to the site where his family was massacred with Kroeber to help Kroeber document Yahi life. Ishi's narrative became Kroeber's narrative, and Kroeber's growing fame became dependent on Ishi.

Ishi struggled in the museum, partly because he was surrounded by the remains of other Native Californians, partly because he was not accustomed to living indoors or wearing Western clothing. He would sometimes be sighted hunting on nearby Mount Parnassus, but for the most part, he was confined to the indoors and forced to essentially be a living exhibit. By many accounts, he was friendly, but one can only imagine what he went through psychologically, spending nights surrounded by the bones of his massacred relatives.

When tuberculosis swept through San Francisco in 1916, Ishi contracted it, probably from one of those curious museum visitors eager to see a live "wild Indian." When he died, Kroeber initially opposed letting Ishi's body be autopsied, but later agreed to have Ishi's brain sent to the Smithsonian, where it remained until 2020.

By then, narratives about Ishi's life had changed. Kroeber's wife, Theodora, also an anthropologist who had studied Native Americans, wrote what was for many years considered the definitive book about Ishi's life, *Ishi in Two Worlds*. But it was an imperfect book in many ways.

Like many Californians, as a child, I was assigned a young reader's version of Theodora Kroeber's book in school, so the Ishi I knew was the Kroeber's Ishi, not the Ishi who belongs to the Native Californians, who would later spend decades fighting to reclaim Ishi's brain so they could lay it to rest with his ashes. And among the stories of Ishi that the Kroebers created, which has remained mythological, is that he was the "last" Native American living wild in California, which is clearly not true: the descendants of many of those Indians who ran from Serra still live here today.

Even while it acknowledged the genocide of Native Americans and grappled with the trauma Ishi experienced when his family was massacred, Theodora Kroeber's book also contributed to the mythology of the "healed" Native American, the person who has been tortured but still manages to be mystically able to move past pain and into forgiveness. Kroeber divides her book into two sections, "The Terror," for Ishi's life before he arrived at the museum, and "The Healing," for the few years he had left once he got there.

Much like the later mythology that forced the survivors of the Charleston Church massacre in 2015 to perform forgiveness to Dylan Roof even if they didn't fully feel forgiving, Native Americans have been forced to conform to mystical, mythical stereotypes, being portrayed in film and television as purified by their people's suffering, shamanic presences capable of healing our broken world.

But the narrative is obviously much more complicated. Ishi will never be able to tell us if he forgave the people who slaughtered his family, if he forgave the supposedly well-meaning white anthropologists who placed him in a museum and exploited his story, if he forgave Serra and gold prospectors and everyone else who has tried to reinvent California in their own image. Ishi will not even be able to tell us his real name because it could only be spoken by another Yahi, and they are gone. The remains of Native people that so bothered Ishi when he lived at the anthropology museum were moved, along with the rest of the museum, to the UC Berkeley campus soon after Ishi died. Tens of thousands of students, faculty, and staff sit in classrooms and offices built over containers of those remains.

In 2015, despite protests from Native American people, Pope Francis canonized Junipero Serra in Washington, DC. The pope described Serra as "excited" about learning Native customs and ways of life, but Native Americans disagreed. Five years later, as statues of Confederate generals, Christopher Columbus, and other disgraced historical figures were being toppled across the country in the wake of the Black Lives Matter movement, Native activists knocked down a thirty-foot-tall statue of Serra in San Francisco's Golden Gate Park. Statues of Serra soon fell in Sacramento and Los Angeles as well. California governor Gavin Newsom had delivered a formal apology to California Native people in 2019, recognizing the history of genocide in the state. But for Native activist Morning

Star Gali, "an apology is nothing without action," and for her and other California Native people, statues of Serra were a reminder of a painful past and needed to go.

The Catholic Church disagreed. San Francisco archbishop Salvatore Cordileone did not apologize to Native activists for the damage the church had done to them throughout history. Instead, he called the activists a "mob," accused them of "an act of sacrilege," and called toppling the statue blasphemy. Cordileone performed an exorcism at the site of the statue, with his own film crew on hand; documenting the ceremony on YouTube; saying, "evil has been done here"; and calling Serra a hero. The statue, depicting Serra thrusting a cross forward with his arms spread wide, now dented and splattered with red paint, has been put in storage. The California legislature voted to replace it with a statue honoring Native Californians. To this day, that statue still does not exist.

***

In July of 2022, Pope Francis, mostly confined to a wheelchair by knee problems, made what the Vatican described as a "penitential pilgrimage" to Canada. The history of Canadian residential schools became an international scandal as reports of thousands of unmarked graves on the sites of former schools became public. Formed by missionaries from Catholic and Protestant denominations on the premise that they would educate First Nations children, Canadian residential schools instead performed what many Native people consider cultural genocide.

Effectively stealing First Nations children from their parents in many cases, missionaries who ran residential schools sexually, physically, and psychologically abused generations of Native Canadian children. And they learned how to do this from their American neighbors. Nicholas Flood Davin, a Canadian politician sent to the USA to study "industrial schools" for Native Americans, wrote in 1897 that "if anything is to be done with the Indian, we must catch him young." To achieve the "aggressive civilization" desired by these politicians, missionaries separated siblings in the schools, weakening family ties, and stuck needles into the tongues of children caught speaking their indigenous languages.

First Nations religions, languages, and cultures were decimated, and untold numbers of children died in residential schools. One report from 1907 estimated a quarter of previously healthy children died in the schools. And anywhere between half and three quarters of those sent to residential schools later died from suicide, addiction, or violence. Residential schools still existed as recently as 1996, and the first apology for the Canadian government's part in them occurred in 2008, when Stephen Harper, then the Prime Minister, offered a public apology before an audience of First Nations people. "The Government of Canada," Harper said, "sincerely apologizes and asks the forgiveness of the Aboriginal peoples of this country for failing them so profoundly." Loraine Yuzicapi, who had been sent to a residential school in the 1950s and sat in the audience as Harper apologized, had a succinct response to a journalist's question about Harper's apology. "It wasn't good enough."

For people who were enslaved or colonized and for their descendants, our growing understanding of epigenetics and trauma theory backs up what they have long said: apologies are not enough to earn forgiveness, because violence, whether mental, physical, or spiritual, can do damage that lasts for generations. Residential schools may have been formed for what their founders saw as a meaningful purpose, the assimilation of Indigenous people into white society and the salvation of their souls through forced conversions to Christianity, but anyone with even a cursory knowledge of missionary history is aware that white supremacy and Eurocentric ideals of "civilization" are what really shaped those missions.

By the time Pope Francis arrived in Canada, First Nations people were understandingly skeptical. Calling the residential schools a "disastrous error" and "catastrophic," the pope also said he humbly begged forgiveness "for the evil committed against the Indigenous peoples." But the pope also said missionaries were acting on behalf of the government, what he described as the "colonizing mentality." Pope Francis did not ask forgiveness for the Catholic Church itself but for its members who abused children. In doing so, the pope perpetuated the same patterns that made the abuse crisis possible.

By pointing the finger at individuals rather than the institution that enabled and even encouraged them, churches and governments alike involved in the residential schools have used the same "bad apples" excuse for generations. The problem is that this effectively allows the institution to call itself blameless. And that in turn increases the potential for the same abuses to happen again.

Murray Sinclair, an Ojibwe Canadian senator and the former head of Canada's Truth and Reconciliation commission, said that this deflection made the pope's apology feel hollow. According to Sinclair, the pope's apology "left a deep hole in the acknowledgement of the full role of the church in the residential school system, by placing blame on individual members of the church." For Sinclair and many other First Nations people who still carry the legacy of trauma and genocide today, the pope's apology was too little, too late. Forgiveness was not granted.

When we talk about apologies and forgiveness, much of our focus is on forgiveness as an unburdening for the person who's done wrong. Once someone is absolved, they are now free to go about their lives. But for the person being asked for forgiveness, absolution is not always possible. It's also, in fact, adding yet another burden for a person who is already carrying the burden of the behavior that injured them, whether psychologically or physically. Because the offender offers an apology with the expectation of forgiveness and its ensuing freedom, when forgiveness is not offered or not possible, sometimes the result is increased resentment on behalf of the violator. We don't know how Pope Francis felt when some of the people he spoke to in Canada later said they felt like his apologies rang hollow or weren't enough. But we do know it's unlikely given his age and health that he'll visit Canada again. The story, for him, was effectively over as soon as his plane touched down in Rome. For the First Nations people, it is not.

***

In his book *The Body Keeps the Score*, psychiatrist Bessel van der Kolk writes that for the traumatized person, "the past is alive in the form of gnawing interior discomfort." Physical aftereffects of trauma become "visceral warning signs," and survivors of trauma "become expert at ignoring their gut feelings and in numbing awareness of what is played out inside." Van der Kolk's hypothesis is that this is another form of the fight or flight instinct experienced by people with anxiety and panic disorders. Because they've experienced trauma, they never feel safe, and as van der Kolk writes, "Being able to feel safe with other people is probably the single most important aspect of mental health."

But since we know America is not a safe country for most women, people of color, queer people, or, increasingly, children at risk of being caught up in a school shooting, the question remains whether America, as a nation that has inflicted trauma on generations of people, is worthy of forgiveness. Of course, America is made up of individuals, and it is individuals who usually ask for forgiveness. But oftentimes, an individual person apologizing on behalf of an institution creates a sense of pressure and stress on the people being apologized to. If forgiveness is expected and pressured out of someone, can its granting ever be genuine?

In an article in *Indian Country* magazine, Dina Gilio-Whitaker, a member of the Colville tribe, writes about attending a production of a play by a Native American writer. The play posed the question of whether or not Native Americans can forgive what was done to them by the United States, and at the end of the play, a non-Native audience member turned to Gilio-Whitaker and said, "You have to forgive if you want to heal." Gilio-Witaker, who says that she experienced domestic abuse, writes that granting forgiveness was not what she personally needed to overcome trauma. She needed to get away from the abuser. She adds that being taught that forgiveness was the only way to move past the abuse perpetuates a victim mentality for abuse survivors because they can be stuck in a perpetual experience of trauma while the abuser moves on.

On a collective level, after a war or genocide, communities "face the extremely challenging prospects of having to rebuild their communities" while also coping with the psychological impact of violence. Furthermore, after a violent conflict, people on both sides have to find a way to exist alongside one another. Instead of asking people stuck together in the aftermath of historical violence whether they can forgive, Gilio-Whitaker suggests a better question: What will it take to heal historical wounds and "heal the relationships between indigenous communities and settler governments and societies?" If we can move past an expectation of forgiveness, she writes, the oppressed are no longer "held to an impossible standard," and we can also recognize that healing is a shared responsibility, not an individual one.

Perhaps if we can let go of the idea that forgiveness might be possible after something as unfathomable as a genocide, war, incest, domestic abuse, rape, or a million other traumatizing acts, we might also be able to let victims and their descendants experience a sense of freedom since they no longer "owe" anyone. Rev. Eric Atcheson, an Armenian American whose ancestors survived the Armenian genocide, told me that he doesn't see it as his or any other Armenian person's responsibility to be forgiving, because the people who could have done this are now dead.

"If God wants to forgive culprits of a genocide," he says, "that's God's affair. I don't get to forgive them in my ancestors' stead." Rev. Atcheson adds that those who accuse the descendants of genocide or war to be "clinging to the past" by refusing to forgive are incorrect. In refusing to forgive or forget the Armenian genocide, Atcheson is "setting [himself] free while the deniers remain burdened." In many ways, this makes perfect sense. We are taught that forgiveness is an unburdening and a letting go, but what if realizing you cannot forgive someone or something is the actual unburdening? As Atcheson says, if it's God's decision whether someone is forgiven, that can free us of the guilt of feeling like we are somehow bad people when we cannot do the same.

And to reduce any group of people to their experience of suffering is also a form of dehumanization. It's amazing to read that Ishi laughed, told people jokes, and enjoyed walking around San Francisco and meeting people, considering his entire family was massacred while he watched. That doesn't necessarily mean he was forgiving but that like every other human being, he felt a range of emotions that extended beyond trauma and its impacts on him. But he also continued to speak Yahi, to practice his tribal rituals, to hunt and carve arrowheads. Living in the museum may have felt like a trap, but when Krober wanted to take Ishi back to his home territory, Ishi did not want to go. To return meant returning to the site of the trauma. Like many other people, he was caught in a liminal space, and that is where he died.

To imagine Ishi or any person who survived a mass slaughter laughing or smiling may tempt us to think they have "let go," forgiven, or moved on. But anyone who's been to a funeral knows that sometimes you laugh hard at funerals because this, too, is a release. That's not the same as moving on or moving past something but a momentary opportunity to feel something other than anxiety or grief. The person being asked for forgiveness, as Gilio-Whitaker writes, is also being "held to an impossible standard." That, too, is turning human suffering into caricature, the "noble savage," the rape victim so holy she is willing to forgive the man who violated her, or the formerly enslaved person who somehow forgives the person who owned their body.

If we are called to be forgiving no matter what, many of us who have been through hell will fail. Perhaps what needs to be forgiven is, instead, the expectation that forgiveness should always be granted.

5

The Epicenter

How the Catholic Church Lost
Its Right to Forgiveness

In March of 2019, the Catholic archbishop of Hartford, Connecticut, decided that a dramatic public statement needed to be made about the forty-eight priests in his diocese who had been accused of sexual abuse. Archbishop Blair held a special "Mass of Reparations" during which he told the congregation that he was there to ask forgiveness, "especially of all the victims of sexual abuse and their families. I ask it for all the Church leadership has done or failed to do," and he prostrated himself in a gesture of repentance. It was a vivid moment that received national press attention. But for many victims and their allies, it was just that: a moment.

For decades, leaders of Catholic dioceses throughout the United States have had to embark on what can only be described as apology tours, during which clergy have again and again asked abuse victims for forgiveness. Nick Ingala, from the lay activist group Voice of the Faithful, told the *New York Times* that Archbishop Blair's Reparations Mass was not going to be enough for many victims. "Apologies," Ingala said, "will only go so far. Where is the responsibility? The accountability? You can't say 'I'm sorry' over and over and over again." Among the reader comments on the *New York Times* article, one of the most upvoted was from "Janet," who stated that "apologies are fine," but that "nothing, absolutely nothing, ever compensates enough for the heart-heavy, dirty-soul feeling that remains with [victims] until we die."

While clergy abuse is not my primary focus in my work as a journalist who writes about the Catholic Church, it is one that my colleagues and I have been forced to return to many times as continued revelations of abuse surface. In fact, every person who writes about the Catholic Church is a de facto reporter on abuse. Journalists often become victim advocates simply because we are the first people victims think to contact, especially when distrust of diocesan offices and the church hierarchy is at an all-time high.

But in spite of the many cases of abuse coming to light around the world, the clerical impulse to plead for forgiveness, and what that does to victims, have rarely been discussed. In 2018, I pitched a story on the role of forgiveness in clergy abuse to a Catholic magazine for which I occasionally write. My hunch was that, like many of the women who were being asked to forgive abusive men as

#MeToo revelations unfolded, many victims of clergy abuse might be hesitant to grant forgiveness to those who had violated them because of the corrosive nature of trauma.

Assuming that Catholics had written widely on clergy forgiveness, I spent a month researching the article. Yet I struggled to find any Catholic sources that specifically addressed what clergy abuse victims should do when the church asks them for forgiveness. In fact, I found nothing. The experience left me wondering why Catholics talk so much about forgiveness without a deeper conversation about what forgiveness means for victims of clergy sexual abuse.

***

There's no statistical information available to show how many victims forgive their abusers, nor do we really know how many abusers ask for forgiveness. Given the layers of secrecy and shame around abuse, those statistics may never emerge. During Pope Francis's apology tour of Canada, the fact that there were hidden graveyards filled with the bones of abuse victims was widely known, but living survivors of the Canadian residential schools have talked extensively about living with shame and secrets for most of their lives. The dead cannot forgive—do the living have to?

In 2018, I was a guest with Rabbi Danya Ruttenberg on an episode of the Canadian Broadcasting Company religion radio show *Tapestry* to discuss forgiveness. Rabbi Ruttenberg said that missing from most discussions of forgiveness are conversations about atonement and making amends. In the context of clergy sexual abuse, atonement can range from financial reparations to abusers entering therapy. Before discussions of forgiveness can begin, according to Rabbi Ruttenberg, the abuser and the institution they belong to both need to demonstrate that there is no chance they will abuse again. This process is neither quick nor easy. And it is the opposite of how the Catholic Church has typically handled abusive priests and bishops.

Atonement is the first step toward understanding that survivors do not, in fact, owe abusers anything. To atone means offering some form of reparations for a wrongdoing, but due to a clerical culture that often casts clergy as superior to the people they serve and therefore untouchable, there has historically been little atonement offered to victims beyond cash payments, if they even receive those. The idea that clergy abusers should be able to ask for forgiveness and then jump back into a clerical office is one that could further damage victims. Yet most of the clerics in the Catholic Church were allowed right back into situations where they continued their abuse. Victims, retraumatized after learning that their abusers also abused others, cannot in fact do enough healing to be capable of forgiveness because atonement never happened. Expecting people to grant forgiveness to an institution that hasn't made legitimate amends does not suggest that institution is capable of real change.

The history of abuse in the Catholic Church is well documented. For centuries, clergy used orphanages, schools, youth groups, and confessionals as cover for sexual, emotional, and spiritual abuse of children and adults alike. The Boston Globe's Spotlight story in 2002 about abuse in the diocese began with an investigation of a single priest who was quietly moved around when he abused children. By the end of the following year, the Globe team had published six hundred more articles on abuse.

Beyond shock at the sheer numbers of abuse cases they'd uncovered, the reporters—several of whom were raised Catholic themselves—were appalled at the ways the church was able to keep this abuse out of the public eye. Walter Robinson, one of the original Spotlight reporters, told the *New Yorker* that nowhere in the documents tracking the shuffling around of abusive clergy was there "any indication anywhere of concern about the children who had been harmed. Not anywhere. It was all about protecting the reputation of the church. It was always about the secrecy."

The psychological companion to secrecy is shame. Psychologists who work with victims of child sexual abuse characterize shame as a "maladaptive emotion" leading to self-blame, vulnerability, and a sense of worthlessness. Shame from sexual abuse has also been described as a "sickness of the soul," a definition that would surely resonate with victims of clergy abuse. People who experience shame as the result of sexual abuse have higher rates of substance abuse, suicidal ideation, and isolation.

In their article "Blame and Shame in Sexual Assault," Prachi Bhupani and Terri Messman-Moore write that "no other trauma group are blamed for their ordeal as frequently as sexual assault victims." Victim-blaming is not new; sexual abuse victims have for centuries been questioned as to why they went to that party, found themselves alone in that room, or kept attending that church. When it comes to children and young people, the shame is often compounded by a lack of understanding that what was happening was, in fact, wrong. A child often does not have language for physical abuse, and because children tend to be trusting of adults, the shame will often become entangled with their sexual development, causing them to have a fear of intimacy as adults that can be difficult to overcome. Even adults who experience sexual abuse often describe the same sense of shame, self-blame, and social stigma.

In addition to victim-blaming, abuse survivors who report on their abuse can be humiliated further by institutions that refuse to believe them. In the Catholic Church particularly, celibate priests are treated with a special kind of respect, a sense that they are ontologically different from laypeople, that when they consecrate communion or baptize babies, they become the actual hands of God. This, along with an increasingly scarce number of priests, leads to what scholars of the church call clericalism: a sense that clergy are superior to laypeople, who must in turn act as subordinate to them.

For centuries, clericalism has led to abuse of all kinds. Martin Luther wrote in 1520 that Catholic priests "regard the lay-men as though they were no Christians." This sense of clerical specialness and condescension toward the laity has led to many priests becoming self-absorbed and narcissistic. It's also caused what some scholars call "ecclesiolatry"—a devotion to the institutionalized hierarchy of a church that becomes obsessive to the point that any character faults a priest might have are willfully overlooked.

Pope Francis has called clericalism "a perversion" and "the root of many evils in the church," and has cautioned priests that it can cause their vocation to become "a power to be exercised rather than a free and generous service to be given." And yet, clericalism still exists and even thrives. Because there are fewer men entering seminaries than ever before, the shrinking number of Catholic priests in the United States is often treated as beyond reproach. While priests today go through far more extensive psychological screening than ever before, clericalism still leads to physical, emotional, and spiritual abuse in the church.

When it comes to sexual assault, however, the stories from history of the Catholic Church are truly horrific. Everything from the Canadian residential schools to the Magdalen laundries in Ireland is an appalling testimony to what happens when clergy are allowed to act with unchecked power. And it was not until recently that the church was willing to apologize for this history. Whether or not the church has atoned for these abuses is up for debate. But in terms of the church even beginning to admit its history of wrongdoing, it wasn't until the Second Vatican Council in the mid-1960s that the church dedicated itself to "aggiornamento," the Italian word for "openness," which became a term the council fathers used to describe the church bringing itself up-to-date by saying Mass in the vernacular languages of the people instead of Latin, changing the worship service to make it more participatory, and offering more transparency from a church that was historically obsessed with secrecy and mystery. This openness also resulted in Vatican documents like *Nostra aetate*, which effectively apologized for blaming Jewish people for Jesus's death and worked to repair relationships with Muslims, who had been punished during the crusades. Aside from those issues, however, Vatican II did not address clergy abuse. It was, at that juncture, still mostly a secret.

The reaction to the Boston story from the church was, of course, indicative that "aggiornamento" only went so far. Cardinal Bernard Law, who led the Boston diocese during the years abusive priests were moved around and who orchestrated the coverup of abuse, was pressed into resigning from his position in Boston. He apologized, and he told clergy abuse victims that he begged their forgiveness. But any hopes abuse survivors had of Law atoning for his wrongdoings were soon dashed. Instead of being demoted, Law was sent to Rome, where he served on numerous papal councils and was named the archpriest of a major Roman basilica. He kept a high profile in Rome and was widely considered influential in the conservative wing of the church. When Law died in 2017, Pope Francis administered rites at the Mass. It was hardly a comedown in status.

The story of abusive priests being promoted instead of demoted isn't uncommon. In 2016, I was part of an international group of journalists who spent two weeks in Rome and at the Vatican meeting cardinals, bishops, and priests; visiting Vatican offices; attending classes and seminars at one of the Pontifical colleges; and learning about reporting on the church. Among the clergy we met was Fr. Justin Wachs, an American priest from the diocese of Sioux Falls. We attended a meeting at the congregation for the Doctrine of the Faith, the Vatican office that oversees cases of abuse. This is where Fr. Wachs worked.

Fr. Wachs told us he'd been assigned to Rome from Sioux Falls because of his expertise in canon law. What he did not tell us was that he'd been assigned there after his parish secretary had accused him of abuse that included unwanted and inappropriate touching, and sexually charged texts and emails. When that story broke in 2017, Wachs was removed from the Vatican office. In the reporting on Wachs by KELO in Sioux Falls, Wachs asked the church employee he abused for forgiveness in letters and texts, also calling her his "dear one" and telling her he missed her, even after she had repeatedly asked him to stop contacting her. But in spite of written evidence and testimonies, he also denied her accusations through his lawyer when she reported Wachs to the bishop. The fact that someone in the Vatican sent a group of journalists to meet with this priest who'd been accused of abuse dripped with irony. But it also reflected how shallow requests for forgiveness from clergy can be.

The greatest scandal of all when it comes to clergy abuse in the Catholic Church is, of course, how much Pope Francis's predecessors knew about the scale of the problem and what they did or didn't do about it. Papal apologies were once uncommon since the pope is understood to speak for the church and the church was supposed to be sinless. However, both Pope John Paul II and Pope Benedict issued apologies for clergy abuse. But those same two popes have both been accused of knowing about abusive clergy and failing to do enough to prevent the crisis from escalating.

Pope Benedict was most likely aware of the clergy abuse happening at a boys' school in Bavaria where 231 boys were abused while Benedict's brother was choir director at the school, and while Benedict himself served as the head of the congregation for the Doctrine of the Faith. Beyond Benedict's likely knowledge about the school, he also oversaw every case of a clergy abuse accusation that made it as far as the Vatican. Pope Benedict, retired from the papacy but still living in luxury in Rome, issued an apology but expressed no empathy for the children abused at the school. Thus far, the German diocese has only offered the victims 2,500 euros in reparations, which is right now worth about 2,000 dollars. One German advocate for abuse victims said Benedict's apology was so weak it "destroyed his reputation as a person, as a theologian, and as head of the church."

Pope Francis has tried to rectify this history by apologizing for church scandals throughout his papacy. According to Annie Selak of Georgetown University, papal apologies "may not say everything, but they say something important." In the past, popes did not apologize on behalf of the church because, according to Selak, that would make the church itself appear sinful. But in a church where the pope's authority is traced back to Jesus's appointment of St. Peter as the leader of the church, today, there's an understanding that because of that lineage, the pope can in fact apologize for actions the church committed in the past.

But some of the popes who very likely knew about clergy abuse have been declared saints, including John Paul II, who was canonized in 2014. Considering he died in 2005, his path to sainthood was astonishingly swift given that the Vatican has taken centuries to canonize many saints. But his canonization wasn't without criticism. Particularly, survivors of clergy sexual abuse and their advocates were vocal about John Paul II's role in the abuse crisis. There are two prominent cases of abuse that took place during his papacy that reflect both the Vatican's propensity to look the other way when abusers have a high profile in the church and reflect some abusers' stubborn refusal to admit what they have done wrong. In the Catholic sacrament of reconciliation, admitting your sins is the first step toward being forgiven. So, what happens when Catholic clergy deny their own wrongdoing?

Father Maciel Macio Delgado was the founder of a Catholic order called the Legion of Christ. Born in Mexico in 1920, as an adult, Maciel presented himself as both an archconservative and defender of orthodoxy and as an enemy of communism. Maciel came from a distinguished church family; four of his uncles were bishops. But he was expelled from multiple seminaries for what he called "misunderstandings." When he was finally ordained, he proved very good at raising money and at keeping secrets, a lethal combination for the men who entered the religious order he founded.

Within the Legion of Christ, Maciel was known as "Nuestro Padre" (Our Father). The Legion taught seminarians that he was a living saint, and they created a lay order called Regnum Christi, which ran the Legion's prep schools, many of which produced young men who would join the Legion. Regnum Christi, too, proved very good at raising money, but it was also a secretive organization, revolving around Delgado in a cult of personality that created the perfect environment for abuse. As far back as 1976, a seminarian who had been abused by Maciel starting at the age of twelve wrote to a bishop about the abuse, and the bishop wrote to the Vatican, suggesting an investigation be opened. In 1978, when John Paul

II became pope, the seminarian and the bishop once again wrote asking for an investigation. There wasn't one.

Maciel was an expert at greasing palms. Legionary seminarians in Rome would make the rounds of prominent Vatican officials' homes every Christmas, delivering gifts of wine and Spanish hams. Cash payments to Vatican officials in exchange for support for the Legion were also apparently common. A recording of John Paul II praising and embracing Maciel was circulated on videotape to Legion supporters, who gave so much money that the order had a billion dollars in assets in the early 2000s. But one newspaper investigation in 1997 had already discovered some of Maciel's history of abuse. Maciel denied it, and the Legion accused the newspaper of fomenting a conspiracy against him. By then, however, Maciel had also fathered multiple children by several different women and had sexually abused at least one of his own sons. He had even once invited one of his own sons to a private Mass with John Paul II. In 2006, after a video tape of Maciel with one of his mistresses and children found its way to the Vatican, Pope Benedict finally banished Maciel to a life of prayer and penance, and Maciel died two years later.

For years, Legionaries had smeared victims of Maciel's abuse as part of a conspiracy. After his death, they were forced to apologize on his behalf because he never admitted he did anything wrong. An investigation later found that 175 minors were abused by 33 priests in the order between 1941 and 2019, and fully a third of those minors were abused by Maciel himself. Maciel fathered at least six children, and one report states that Maciel's elder sons tried to prevent his younger sons from being left alone with him because he would abuse his own children given the opportunity.

But Maciel not only refused to apologize for doing anything wrong; he flatly denied it. In 2002, he said, "I never engaged in the sort of repulsive behavior these men accuse me of." John Paul II, stricken with Parkinson's disease, died in 2005 before Maciel was forced out of the priesthood, but not before public reports about his abuse began to surface. But while John Paul II would send apologies to some victims of clergy abuse, he never authorized an investigation of Maciel and continued to see the Legion as a success story until he died.

This same propensity to look the other way would be part of John Paul II's tainted legacy when it came to another prominent Catholic, Cardinal Theodore McCarrick. Unlike Maciel, whose order drew praise from prominent conservative Catholics, McCarrick was a more moderate or even liberal face of Catholicism. He presided at the funerals of Ted Kennedy and Joe Biden's son Beau, posed for photos with Bono from the band U2, and frequently appeared on television, offering commentary on social justice issues and the abuse crisis. The latter role McCarrick played in the media as the friendly explainer of where the church went wrong with abuse would become highly ironic.

After serving as the Archbishop of Newark, McCarrick was made Archbishop of Washington, DC, by Pope John Paul II in 2000. Like Maciel, he was charismatic, charming, and good at fundraising and making connections. Even after his retirement, he continued to travel widely and to lobby for immigrant rights, to meet with victims of natural disasters, and to serve as a media commentator on church issues. But for decades, McCarrick had used his position to abuse seminarians, inviting them to his beach house, where he'd ask them to join him in bed. He went as far as to refer to these young men as his "nephews" and signed letters to them as "Uncle Ted." Rumors about McCarrick's treatment of seminarians had swirled for decades, and according to the *New York Times*, at least one priest warned the Vatican against John Paul II's promotion of him to Archbishop of Washington, DC. But John Paul II had overlooked rumors about Maciel, and he seems to have done the same with McCarrick.

It is rare that a bishop is defrocked in the Catholic Church. However, that's what happened to McCarrick in 2019. In the face of public pressure to crack down on abuse, McCarrick was not only stripped of his ecclesial titles but also sent to a small town in Kansas to live in a house run by Capuchin Franciscans. The town wasn't happy about this since the friary was close to an elementary school. Ruth Graham, who was reporting for *Slate* at the time, traveled to Kansas and was able to interview McCarrick for the first time since his defrocking. An elderly and increasingly frail McCarrick denied everything. According to Graham,

> I asked him if he had done it. He has been accused of sexually assaulting minors and making unwanted advances on seminary students he invited to his beach house in New Jersey over the course of many decades. Were those stories true? "I'm not as bad as they paint me," he said. "I do not believe that I did the things that they accused me of." I told him it sounded like he

thought it was possible—that saying he didn't "believe" he had done those things, or that he doesn't remember them, makes it sound as if he's leaving it an open question. No, he said.

When Graham pressed him about this further, McCarrick stated that many seminarians had visited the beach house and not had an issue, so how could he be guilty? And when she asked who might have framed him if he wasn't guilty, McCarrick could only vaguely refer to "enemies."

For years, the Legion of Christ similarly denied accusations that Maciel had abused anyone by also framing the accusations as the work of a shadowy cabal of "enemies." But eventually, the Legion had to apologize on behalf of Maciel. McCarrick, however, has never done that. In his 2018 statement to the media, he wrote, "While I have absolutely no recollection of this reported abuse, and believe in my innocence, I am sorry for the pain the person who brought these charges has gone through." This is not actually an apology because it fails to admit any wrongdoing. But a 2020 investigation released by the Vatican secretary of state included 450 pages of stories of the church's repeated failures to stop McCarrick from abusing people. McCarrick may have denied he did anything, but the facts told a different story.

"There were so many opportunities to stop him," John Bellochio, who is suing both McCarrick and the Holy See, told the Associated Press. "Maybe my life would be different, maybe I wouldn't be a victim if someone had." Geoffery Downs, who accused McCarrick of abusing him while he was still an altar boy, added that reading the Vatican report "is crushing to those of us who went through it because you realize how small and incidental you are to these creatures, predators." James Grein, who came forward in 2018 and accused McCarrick of abusing him for two decades, said that the abuse had led to suicidal thoughts, alcoholism, and post-traumatic stress. "How they could ever repair my damage," Grein said, "I don't know."

None of this sounds like forgiveness. McCarrick, who is ninety-two as I write this, has been arraigned by a court in Massachusetts, but the trial has yet to begin. Adam A. J. DeVille, a psychologist who teaches at the University of St. Francis, wrote in *Commonweal Magazine* that seeing the stooped and frail McCarrick entering a courtroom failed to raise any sense of pity, even though DeVille works with sexual predators in his practice as a psychologist. DeVille, a Catholic, writes that our temptation is to wonder if sex offenders who prey on children in particular "would be better off dead." However, he says, "facile demonization is not permitted to Christians or clinicians."

DeVille writes that as a psychologist, his task is to "never reduce a human being to some neat category." To make progress and prevent themselves from offending again, sex offenders need to examine what they've done—to examine it, repent of it, and seek forgiveness for it. "Good psychotherapy," DeVille writes, "must be about challenging people to change." For Catholics who revile predators like McCarrick, according to DeVille, forgiveness should not be demanded of anyone and it can only be given by victims, and only on their own timeline. DeVille then challenges the reader to consider what forgiveness can do when it is freely offered.

Forgiveness breaks deathly cycles of destruction and recrimination, at least some of the time and in some ways. And real forgiveness is capacious enough that it does not require uniformity of practice. It does not require that we ever again like or be close to a person who has done evil to us. Nor is it necessarily completed in one discrete action; it may gradually unfold over time. A forgiving people can at the same time be revolted by an abuser's actions, demand that he face justice and make reparations to his victims, insist he be permanently ejected from all positions in the Church, work tirelessly to overthrow the corrupt systems that allowed him to get away with his abuse for so long—and *also* love him as a fallen human being and a child of the merciful God who saw his own son sadistically abused, humiliated, and killed.

This concept of forgiveness, unlike the idea of forgive and forget, hinges on the idea that the institution that enables the abuse should be held accountable, which has not always happened in the case of the Catholic Church. However, most people who have been the victims of serial predators like McCarrick could work very hard with a skilled psychotherapist and still struggle to "love him as a fallen human being." This is, perhaps, what being a believer demands of us, but there is a reason many victims of clergy abuse have turned their backs on organized religion.

At this juncture, I should probably admit that this is a personal story. I'm not simply a journalist who covers the Catholic Church. I'm also a survivor of sexual abuse. Although I was never abused by clergy, an abusive incident took place near the Catholic elementary school I attended. The person was never found, and it's likely they went on to abuse more children. For me, this issue is so important because I have experienced it firsthand and know what kind of consequences are involved for victims.

I often think of Jesus's crucifixion scene as the root of our incomplete understanding of forgiveness in the Catholic Church. In the Gospel of Luke, Christ looks down on his killers and says, "Father forgive them, for they know not what they do." But in the case of the cardinals and bishops and the popes who knew—who heard and saw what abusers were doing and relocated them or covered things up—and for the priests and nuns who knew—who knew about their colleagues' abuses and did not tell, or who were abusers themselves—forced forgiveness could be seen as a form of spiritual abuse.

The church can write checks to its heart's content, bankrupt dioceses, stage Reparation Masses, build "healing gardens," and beg for forgiveness. But until it owns up to the fact that it has not allowed adequate space for victims to express themselves, confront their abusers, and thus begin to heal, no true acts of atonement have been performed. As of today, there is still no evidence that victims owe the church any forgiveness. The Catholic Church has repeatedly chosen to protect the institution at the victims' expense. Asking victims to forgive an institution so deeply corrupted also asks them to relive horrific and painful experiences not for their own sake but for the sake of their abusers who need to "move on."

Many of us who write about abuse do so because we are believers ourselves, and for us, this is an issue of justice. We strive to do this work not with pity, which is looking down on someone, but with empathy, which is moving into another person's pain. This is the same understanding that helps us to know, according to the Catholic tradition, that only a God who suffers with victims can be capable of offering any kind of forgiveness, because God takes on the burden and does the work of forgiving on our behalf. In a theology that centers victims' experiences, forgiveness should be in the hands of a God who suffers, not a responsibility resting on the shoulders of those who have been abused.

6

Evangelical Forgiveness and Spiritual Abuse

In March of 2022, the American Evangelical flagship magazine *Christianity Today* shocked thousands of people by dropping a surprise story in which *Christianity Today* reporter Daniel Silliman revealed that, for over twelve years, female employees had experienced sexual harassment at *Christianity Today* from former editor-in-chief Mark Galli and former advertising director Olatokunbo Olawoye. According to then-current editor Timothy Dalrymple, Silliman was invited to write this investigation by the magazine's editors. At the recommendation of abuse victim and attorney Rachel Denhollander, *Christianity Today* also hired Guidepost Solutions, a business consulting company, to investigate the abuse claims and make recommendations. Silliman did not see the Guidepost report until after he had concluded his own reporting. The magazine, according to both Silliman's article and Guidepost Solution's report, had done little if anything to mitigate the abuse.

The story of how all this unfolded is highly unusual in journalism. Unlike the *Boston Globe* reporting on clergy abuse in the Catholic Church, the timing and circumstances of both *Christianity Today*'s reports surfacing at once was curious. Oftentimes, when an institution reports on its own failings, it is doing a form of public relations to get ahead of and shape the story before an outsider reveals the unvarnished problems.

Christianity Today, founded by Billy Graham in the 1950s, has had a large readership, making it a powerful voice for conservative Protestant values around issues of sex and sexuality. It has also been primarily led by men, and, statistically, men are far more likely to sexually harass women than vice versa. The response to Silliman's report that female staffers were groped and verbally abused was explosive on social media. Even in the post-Trump era, white Evangelical culture remains a subject of fascination for many outside of it.

Unlike the Catholic Church, where abuse cases must at least theoretically be reported to central bodies like diocesan offices, Evangelical churches have no center of power akin to Rome, and there is often no one like a bishop supervising the behavior of pastors. Often there is little or no accountability for pastors beyond their congregations, and those pastors wield incredible power over their congregations' ideas about forgiveness.

Matthew Boedy, a writer and professor who studies the rhetoric of religion, grew up as an Evangelical and remained one for many years of his adult life. When a pastor at a church plant—a newly formed Evangelical church where the pastor is often the sole leader and answers to no one above them—crossed boundaries in Boedy's relationship with his therapist and his wife, Boedy was effectively excommunicated by the pastor. Boedy told me this was because had what the church called "an unforgiving spirit" after refusing to forgive a spiritual abuser. In other words," he continues, "the demand for forgiveness of an act the abuser didn't see as sin was quick, and when I didn't comply, I was banished."

Boedy, who wrote about the pastor at a blog that exposes spiritual abuse and is working on a book about trauma and rhetoric, says, "I can say from personal and professional experience, the demand for forgiveness of abuse of any kind is quicker and stronger in Evangelical churches compared to others because the abusers often are in power in an intimate or small church setting and want to keep that power." Self-protection, in other words, is more important to many Evangelical leaders than the lives of their congregations. Boedy adds that "demand for quick forgiveness to them isn't a sign of deep guilt but a sign of tremendous power."

There is also an emphasis among many Evangelicals that forgiveness has to be swift, which means the idea that it should be a process including accountability or reconciliation is not really possible. In an essay at the website of The Gospel Coalition, a network of Evangelical churches, David VanDrunen writes of forgiveness that "there is no turning point in a person's life more important than when she goes from being under God's condemnation to enjoying his favor, from being on the road to hell to becoming an heir of heaven. The forgiveness of sins through justification by faith is what marks this turning point." The emphasis on forgiveness taking place in a moment and only requiring a person to make a quick decision that will set them on the path to heaven negates the idea of forgiveness involving any kind of interior or collective process that would create accountability on either side. This also means people move swiftly past traumatic events in some Evangelical circles, which can have lasting consequences.

According to writer and former *Christianity Today* editor Katelyn Beaty, a "default posture of grace" and forgiveness among Evangelicals means that disgraced Evangelical pastors and church leaders find it relatively easy to return to positions of power after abuse. Beaty writes that "many evangelicals can't resist a charismatic leader with an amazing redemption story to share or sell," and for many fallen Evangelical pastors and leaders, this redemption story becomes part of their brand. The writer Elizabeth Spiers has even said that Evangelicals have "built in insurance for reputational damage," because pressure to forgive a fallen leader—especially a powerful white male one—means their comebacks are pretty much inevitable. Among Evangelical laypeople, those who refuse forgiveness are, according to Beaty, seen as not only suspicious but as stubbornly standing in the way of grace: they are "just being critical, gossips, believing the worst about others, or part of Satan's plan to prevent God's kingdom plans from unfolding."

Unfortunately, according to Silliman's reporting, this typical Evangelical structure—with a powerful man at the top and everyone else below—was replicated at *Christianity Today*. And powerful men, no matter their religious background, are most concerned with protecting themselves.

In Silliman's report, most of the harassment cases disclosed to human resources were buried or pushed aside, but much of the harassment never even made it to HR. In one disturbing incident, a woman whose sexual harassment was reported to HR by a colleague found herself on the receiving end of a stream of grievances from former editor Mark Galli, who accused her of seeing "everything" as sexual harassment. Amy Jackson, a former associate publisher who left the magazine in 2018 due to what she described as a "hostile work environment," told Silliman that "the culture when I was there was to protect the institution at all costs."

Anyone who remembers Jim Bakker, Jimmy Swaggart, Jerry Falwell Jr., Doug Phillips, or any other name on the long list of Evangelical pastors who were involved in sex scandals knows there is a pattern among powerful Evangelical preachers that often leads to abuse coverups. In addition, the #ChurchToo movement, started by Evangelical women who were victims of abuse, has also made it clear that these patterns of abuse and coverup are more extensive than many people had previously known. The issue at *Christianity Today*, too, seems to be a consistent pattern of denial that anything was wrong. Guidepost Solutions, the consulting firm hired by *Christianity Today*, reported that the publication's "flawed institutional response to harassment allegations could have been influenced, in part, by unconscious sexism," and that some of the problem may have stemmed from older men "out of touch with current workplace mores."

For his part, Galli, who retired from *Christianity Today* in 2019, sounded defensive in an interview with *Religion News Service,* in which Galli claimed that the stories in Silliman's report were "taken out of context" or "simply not true." Galli left Evangelicalism behind when he retired from *Christianity Today*, ironically converting to Catholicism, a denomination with its own history of abuse and denial. Olayowe, on the other hand, was fired by *Christianity Today* in 2017 after being arrested in a sting operation and pleading guilty to meeting a minor for sex. He did three years in prison and now lives as a registered sex offender.

***

When we're thinking about the idea of forgiveness, the *Christianity Today* story leads to two overlapping questions: Who is really at fault here, and should they be expected to seek forgiveness? And in a larger sense, how do Evangelical notions of forgiveness lead to spiritual, sexual, and emotional abuse? In his editor's letter that accompanied Silliman's report, Timothy Dalrymple said the whole process had taken place out of a greater need for transparency. "We owe it to the women involved to say we believe their stories," Dalrymple wrote, "and we are deeply sorry the ministry failed to create an environment in which they were treated with respect and dignity." Dalrymple had just come on board as editor-in-chief when some of these accusations began to surface in 2019, and more women continued to come forward in subsequent years. All evidence seems to indicate a series of miscommunications and a problem with the institutional culture of the magazine and of Evangelicalism rather than responsibility residing with a single person. Dalrymple's apology is straightforward and accompanied by promises for greater accountability. Time will tell how or if that manifests at *Christianity Today*, but Evangelical notions of forgiveness may make maintaining that promised transparency a challenge.

In an interview with *Slate*'s Molly Olmstead after the report was released, Silliman talked about what forgiveness means for Evangelicals like himself. From an Evangelical perspective, Silliman says, "there is an idea that in any kind of personal conflict or disagreement or even harm, the ultimate aim for Christians should be the reconciliation of the two parties." Silliman goes on to say that one of the accused men he reported on seems to believe that "a true Christian should not report stuff if it gets in the way of reconciliation." Journalists who publish such reports, according to this logic, hamper possibilities for forgiveness and reconciliation.

That pattern of blaming members of the media for spending too much time reporting on abuse and too little time focusing on stories of reconciliation is not new and not even a particularly Evangelical pattern. Much like Protestant churches find their roots in Catholicism, the pattern of protecting the institution at all costs is rooted in Catholic history. Back in 2003, now-Archbishop Wilton Gregory, formerly the head of the US Conference of Catholic Bishops, told reporters that while reporting on abuse was helpful in creating more accountability, "the way the story [of abuse] was so obsessively covered resulted in unnecessary damage to the bishops and the entire Catholic community." Gregory neglected to consider that many of those reporters were themselves Catholics and perhaps invested in holding an institution they cared about accountable, much like Silliman.

But a reason reporters might not be focusing on stories of reconciliation between abuse victims and church-led institutions is simply that there are not many stories about reconciliation and forgiveness to tell. In 2022, the Southern Baptist Coalition, America's largest Evangelical denomination, released the results of a multiyear investigation into abuse. In the *Atlantic*, Evangelical writer David French wrote that the report showed that abuse survivors "were ignored, disbelieved, or met with the constant refrain that the SBC could take no action due to its policy regarding church autonomy." The report also revealed that SBC ministers would call abuse victims "opportunistic," and ministers accused victims of wanting to "burn things to the ground."

French asks his readers, "How many times must evangelicals watch powerful institutions promote and protect sexual predators before we acknowledge the obvious crisis?" The reports on the SBC, *Christianity Today*, and the fall of Evangelical superstars like Jerry Falwell Jr. all occurring within a few years of one another should have been catastrophic. But each time, there was enough hubris on the part of the Evangelical institution or individual to trust that they would eventually be forgiven. Very rarely, however, do abuse victims announce that they have granted their forgiveness and are ready to move on. Perhaps that is because forgiveness has not been earned.

***

In June of 2020, the writer Daniel Lavery started a Twitter thread with the following post: "In November of last year, I reported to the Elders of Menlo Church that their senior pastor, John Ortberg, had conspired in secret to provide a person experiencing compulsive sexual feelings towards children with unsupervised access to young people through youth groups." Lavery went on to reveal several key details related to this incident. One was something many readers were aware of, which is that John Ortberg is Lavery's father. The other was that the youth group volunteer who had expressed sexual feelings toward children was John Ortberg Jr., Lavery's younger brother. Menlo Church is a megachurch with a congregation of about five thousand people. It was formerly a member of the PCUSA, a relatively liberal denomination of Presbyterians, but it left the PCUSA under Ortberg's leadership in 2014 after the PCUSA began to be more welcoming of LGBTQ people. Given the size of his father's platform, news of Lavery's statement quickly circulated around the internet.

Before coming to Menlo Church, Ortberg and his wife were pastors at Willow Creek Church, one of America's largest nondenominational megachurches. Bill Hybels, Willow Creek's senior pastor, was removed in 2018 after accusations of his abusing women in the congregation turned out to be true. For Hybels and other megachurch pastors, it's particularly complicated when they're accused of participating in or covering up abuse because the pastor is, according to Laurie Goodstein of the *New York Times*, "the superstar on whom everything else rests, making accusations of harassment especially difficult to confront." And in megachurches independent of denominations, "there is no larger hierarchy to set policies and keep the pastor accountable" because boards of elders are usually volunteers chosen by the pastor. Victims at Evangelical churches are often afraid to come forward because of a fear of damaging the church's ministry, according to Boz Tchividjian, an attorney who leads GRACE, an organization that works with victims of church abuse. As a result, Evangelical leaders often feel hubris to an extreme degree because they and their congregations see them as the hands, feet, and voice of Jesus. "Those leaders feel almost invincible," Tchividjian points out.

In this kind of environment where a pastor's reputation alone is what can make or break a church, congregations can have a propensity to be overly forgiving. If they're not forgiving, the entire enterprise of a beloved church can crumble into dust. Like his mentor Bill Hybels, John Ortberg was by most measures a successful and experienced celebrity pastor: the author of multiple books and a frequent speaker at events like Promise Keepers, which are stadium-sized spiritual rallies for men. According to Bob Smietana's reporting for *Religion News Service*, when Lavery confronted Ortberg with the story John Jr. had shared about his attraction to children, Ortberg told Lavery to keep the story secret and referred to John Jr. as a "virtuous pedophile" because he believed that John Jr. had never acted on the attraction.

Lavery finally decided to report his father to the Menlo Church board. He wrote to them that in choosing to hide their other son's sexual attraction to children even while allowing that son to volunteer with children, "my parents have acted with unconscionable disregard for their responsibilities as leaders, ministers, and parents." The board placed Ortbeg on leave and conducted an investigation, but it only lasted six weeks, and at the end, Ortberg was allowed to return to the pulpit. Lavery expressed skepticism, telling Smietana that "I don't know how you can investigate 16 years of volunteer work in about five weeks over the Christmas holidays."

Frustrated with the shortcomings of the investigation, Lavery posted that Twitter thread six months later, naming his brother as the volunteer his father had protected. In the Twitter thread, Lavery wrote that "parishioners were not given the full story of Ortberg's relationship to this volunteer, or his interest in keeping their strategy a secret." When reports later revealed that Lavery's sister did not feel comfortable leaving her own child alone with John Jr., the pressure on Ortberg to resign increased, and he finally stepped down in July 2020. Ortberg admitted to using "poor judgment" in keeping his son's attraction to children hidden while also allowing him to continue volunteering with them.

The fallout was dramatic, but Lavery felt like he had no other choice. In his newsletter, Lavery wrote that he and his wife, Grace, "knew very well the course of action we were embarking upon would be costly, would invite a great deal of public speculation and harassment, and might very well fail to bring about the thorough investigation, justice, and repair we hoped for." Lavery, who is transgender, took his wife's last name and moved across the country to Brooklyn to put as much distance between himself and his family as possible. Lavery told *Vanity Fair* that coming from an Evangelical family, he felt pressured to hide his transness for as long as possible due to "the potential of abandonment, the sense that anything can be taken away at any moment." Lavery described the final conversation he had with this father in his newsletter, writing that his father was "alternately gentling, reassuring, using language about 'journeys' and complexity, and then in the next moment fierce, adamant, paternal, speaking *ex cathedra*, with a perfect explanation for why secrecy was the only possibility." What his father was not, according to Lavery, was apologetic.

Perhaps Ortberg didn't need to be apologetic because his fellow Evangelical pastors had already forgiven him. By 2022, he was listed as a mentor for "The Ascent," a Christian coaching group. But "replatforming" of pastors who collude in, participate in, or cover up abuse is not new in Evangelical culture. As the Evangelical journalist Julie Roys writes, "There is no true process in evangelicalism for qualifying leaders once they're disqualified. Instead, the compromised leader generally leverages his extraordinary gifting, charisma, and relational capital to gain critical mass. And voilá, he's back." For his part, when he left Menlo Church, Ortberg apologized to the congregation for his mistakes and asked for their forgiveness, but there's no record of him doing the same thing with his son.

The Ortberg family is not the only one where secrecy, patriarchy, and coerced or forced forgiveness combine into a toxic Evangelical stew. The Rev. Carol Howard-Merrit grew up in a Southern Baptist family where her father regularly erupted, a volcano whose rage was fed by the notion that as the head of a "good Christian family," his wife and children must submit to his will. As a girl, Rev. Howard-Merrit knew that their church pastor was a pedophile who preyed on her sister, but her church turned inward to protect the pastor instead of reaching out to help her sister.

This background often leads people to question why she entered the ministry when the Southern Baptist church of her childhood colluded in the violence she grew up surrounded by. In her book *Healing Spiritual Wounds*, she writes that religion was "complicit in the violence" of her home and church, but that she "still searched for spiritual peace." Christianity, she writes, "was part of the problem," but was also her "cure, solace, and center." Over time, she came to understand that abusive patterns in religion "did not really represent God," and after attending Moody Bible Institute, she left the Southern Baptist Church to join the Presbyterian Church (USA), where she was ordained, and where she began a ministry that focuses on religious wounds and spiritual healing.

Spiritual abuse, which can involve forced or coerced forgiveness, is increasingly recognized as common in Evangelical churches with powerful pastors and almost no denominational oversight. Rev. Merritt explains that spiritual abuse is typically "different from physical or psychological abuse. It usually happens when a person isn't able to love or be loved by God." In many cases, this is rooted in an understanding of God as "vengeful, angry or judgmental." Spiritual abuse can also come from "a church that proclaims we are not loved by God or sinful," resulting in people who are not able to love themselves or their neighbor. According to Rev. Merritt, spiritual abuse is also rooted in social structures, such as white supremacy, classism, and sexism, all of which prey on the most vulnerable in society.

The aftermath experiences of victims of spiritual abuse "happens internally," so telling the stories of people she's pastored helped her to frame the experience of spiritual abuse "to think about it more practically." As she writes, the more she worked with abuse victims, the more she saw "patterns in the ways we found healing," which helped her to realize "God was calling [her] to help people to separate religious wounds from their positive experiences with God and to restore the latter."

But complicating the notion of healing or recovery from abuse is the notion that abuse can occur both on an individual and institutional level. Rev. Merritt experienced this personally as the result of her abusive father and her sister's experience of an abusive pastor. In the case of the pastor, "the covering up was a whole other realm of hurt." Some of the process toward healing she describes is "understanding the urge to protect the organization because it serves a higher good." However, that protective urge often happens because of fear that the abused person "might destroy the institution." And, Rev. Merritt says, covering up abuse "goes against how we should be as Christians because of confession and reconciliation."

This pattern of covering up abuse also gets in the way of true reconciliation because the forgiveness asked of victims is often responded to by a lack of willingness to change on the part of the institutional church. According to Kathryn Joyce, who has written about fundamentalist and Evangelical Christian churches for many years, hiding abuse is often tied into notions of authoritarianism. In churches "where there's a heavy emphasis on obedience" and "unquestioning respect toward leaders," there is a pattern of "subsuming the interests of the individual to protect the mission."

But coverups of abuse in many churches are also complicated by patriarchal structures where women and children in particular have almost no agency. According to Joyce, in fundamentalist communities like Quiverfull, the extreme focus on female modesty as a source of temptation to men results in situations like that of a young girl she encountered who was being abused by an older man, "but people were talking about whether or not she was boy crazy and had brought that on."

Sarah Jones, who writes for *New York Magazine* and grew up in a fundamentalist homeschooling family, says this notion of women as tempters is taught from a young age: "You are told God designed you to be submissive, and that your body is a stumbling block to men. These doctrines are not particularly conducive to creating a culture that takes sexual abuse seriously. They instead encourage shame and silence."

Merritt explains that this second-guessing of abuse victims is related to the concept of gaslighting, where a victim is told that what they are experiencing is essentially all in their imagination. Gaslighting, too, can take the form of asking for forgiveness when a person or institution apologizes but also tries to reframe the narrative of what actually happened. "One way in which the church powerfully protects itself," she says, "is by diminishing testimony of victims." Examples of this might include telling the person that "they must have misunderstood" the abuse, questioning their story, or telling them they're lying in subtle ways. All of these actions serve to protect the institution, but at the expense of the victims. Merritt explains that "this becomes spiritual abuse because the person is beginning to believe that God doesn't believe them," and ultimately, they come to see themselves as untrustworthy.

In patriarchal churches, an understanding of God is based on an image of God as "protector and provider, which is sound theology" according to Rev. Merritt. But when abuse occurs, "something breaks down" in the victim's understanding of God. When this extends to a church's theology, it makes women and children more vulnerable to spiritual abuse. This patriarchal version of God also tied up women being told that "their understanding of doctrine can't be trusted, or they have to submit to male authority," which can lead to a crisis of women questioning their own "internal authority."

Kathryn Joyce adds that spiritual abuse can have profoundly alienating effects on women and children brought up in very strict religious environments. She cites the work of Boz Tchividjian, who in addition to being an attorney working with abuse victims happens to be the grandson of Billy Graham. Tchividjian says that abuse is most likely to occur in church settings where there's a heavy emphasis on obedience, which makes it less likely for victims to speak up. In strictly religious families, that often means abuse by a husband, father, or male pastor is brushed off as part of a biblical understanding that the father, even if he is abusive, is always the head of the family, and his behavior cannot be questioned.

Joyce explains that for "devout people, having their faith perverted" by abuse "is extraordinarily painful and can take away one of the most important parts of their lives when they most need it." Organizations like GRACE often find that churches use their religious authority to "coerce victims and survivors" by telling them not to speak up because they will hurt the church or convincing them that have been complicit in the sin. Christians who work on this issue, Joyce says, find this spiritual abuse one of the most harmful aspects of abusive patterns. And Sarah Jones adds that "fundamentalist churches often teach that psychology is a sinful, atheistic profession," another obstacle to victims seeking help.

Rev. Merritt says that part of helping people recover from a broken understanding of God after abuse lies in liberation theology. The image of a God who "suffers with us" can offer more consolation to the abused because that parental God is present in our suffering. Devotions by women to Our Lady of Sorrows, for example, allow abused women to imagine a God who feels the same pain they do. This suffering God helps a victim of spiritual abuse to be "more resilient" because they now have a "suffering parent walking with us and suffering with us." The approach to dealing with spiritual abuse must be pastoral and individual. Victims need to be heard, acknowledged, and understood. And for Evangelical churches in particular, that means powerful pastors need to cede some or all of their power. Only then can the idea that forgiveness must be meted out so that pastors can be re-platformed perhaps begins to change.

This may be an uphill battle. In 2022, it was announced that John Ortberg, still in the process of re-platforming himself, endorsed a book by Andy Stanley, another Evangelical pastor who had begun to issue a somewhat softer tone on LGBTQ people than some "Bible-believing" Evangelicals who preach that all LGBTQ people are condemned. Stanley stated that he wanted to "build bridges" especially between LGBTQ people and their parents, and in 2023, he also announced a conference to help out Evangelical parents of LGBTQ kids, with Ortberg initially listed as one of the speakers. But Ortberg soon disappeared from the lineup. Whether that was pressure from "Bible-believing" Evangelicals or maybe the fact that there's no evidence Ortberg has a healed relationship with his own transgender son, Ortberg seems to have decided it wasn't worth the risk to his reputation. But you can't re-platform without forgiving yourself. And Ortberg seems to have done just that.

For several years, Daniel Lavery wrote an advice column for *Slate* under the "Dear Prudence" header. In 2021, after separating from his family, Lavery replied to a letter from a reader who had been assaulted by her brother. Her family had for years pressured her to forgive the brother, to get over it and move on, even though the brother never apologized and was by most signs unrepentant. Lavery's response to the reader went, in part, like this:

> If you don't want to be around him (especially since he's never attempted to make amends for the way he harmed you), then that's a perfectly sound and sane decision. Anyone who tries to make you feel guilty for that choice is wrong to do so. It may, unfortunately, mean that for at least the time being, you don't spend time with your other siblings or parents either, but you may experience some relief in getting distance from them, too.

7

Bodies

Rape, Abortion, and Forgiveness

In Heather King's memoir of her conversion to Catholicism, *Redeemed*, she writes that she "read of" a film about the Rwandan genocide in which a Tutsi woman was "gang raped so many times she lost count" and then left for dead. This woman, according to King, forgave her rapists. The woman then went on to bear the child of the rape and named the child Akima, Child of God. King, who spends a large part of her book explaining how she went from being pro-choice to opposing abortion, doesn't source this story beyond naming the documentary she read about.

As a journalist, I know that memoirs don't rely on sources as much as they do an author's sometimes fuzzy recollections. So I did some research into King's story. *God Sleeps in Rwanda* is a short documentary made by three women filmmakers in 2004. It was nominated for an Academy Award and toured several well-known film festivals. I found interviews with the filmmakers online in which they mentioned how brutally rape was used as a weapon in Rwanda, how many women who survived it had been diagnosed with AIDS, and how many of them died from it.

And I found the film on YouTube. In it, the woman King mentions says she wanted to have an abortion, but that people advised her not to. Many Rwandans are devout Catholics, and according to the Guttmacher Institute, abortions are extremely difficult to access there, so untold numbers of women had children as the result of rapes during the genocide. She also says that while her child is innocent, she doesn't want her daughter to know that she's the product of rape, so she has not told her daughter how she was conceived.

While this story can be manipulated to sound touching in the hands of a pro-life activist like King, it does not seem like a clear-cut example of forgiveness. In her writing about it, King sweeps over the fact that the woman, like many other Rwandan women, wanted an abortion but could not procure one. The narrative of forgiveness that she crafts serves the purpose of making people feel like Rwandan women who bore these children did so willingly because they were following a moral path. But rape and sexual assault are perhaps uniquely hard to forgive because the person who's experienced them may not know the identity of the person who attacked them, may be living in fear of another assault, or may be afraid of retaliation for reporting the crime if they do know the attacker. There is also a culture of secrecy and shame around rape that prevents many victims from ever coming forward, much less finding their way through the thickets of trauma responses that follow a sexual assault. And religion, Christianity in particular, has fueled much of the shame culture around sexual assault, as well as putting pressure on victims to forgive those who assault them. The pro-life movement has often sought out stories of women who forgave their rapists and bore the child resulting from the rape because it's a convenient narrative. If she could do it, why can't every other rape victim now seeking an abortion be just as forgiving? The answer is much more complicated and less convenient than many would like it to be.

***

In 2009, a Brazilian man raped his nine-year-old stepdaughter, and she became pregnant with twins. Her mother, panicked that her child would die as a result of the pregnancy, arranged for an emergency procedure to terminate the pregnancy. Abortion is illegal in Brazil except in cases of rape and when the mother's life is in danger—both true in this case—and up to 250,000 women a year there end up in emergency rooms because of botched illegal abortion procedures. Brazil's population is more than half Roman Catholic, but even for the most faithful Catholics, what happened next was shocking.

The nine-year-old's hips were so small they would have made the pregnancy dangerous, so an argument could have been made that the Catholic Church would allow the pregnancy to be terminated to save the girl's life because this was a case of "double effect." Double effect is what the thirteenth-century theologian and philosopher Thomas Aquinas referred to as "causing a morally grave harm as a means of pursuing a good end." Technically, under church canon law, anyone who aids in an abortion or participates in one is considered to be excommunicated *latae sententiae*, or automatically. For Catholics, excommunication means a person is banned from taking communion in any church until they go to confession and repent. But the priest or bishop they confess to is ultimately the person who decides whether or not a person is forgiven. However, when a pregnancy is terminated to save the mother's life, as it was in the case of this pregnant child, the church can make an exception and doesn't necessarily consider the mother excommunicated.

Because most abortions are private matters between a person and their doctor, it would be impossible for the church to know who has and hasn't received one. But because the case in Brazil was so appalling, what happened next was international news that still resonates today. Archbishop Sobrinho of the city of Recife excommunicated the girl, her doctors, and her mother. At the time, he told *Time* magazine, "Abortion is more serious than killing an adult." Sobrinho said that anyone who disagreed with the church on his decision was not Catholic and should feel free to leave the church. "We want people who adhere to God's laws," he said.

Catholic teaching on abortion has always been closely intertwined with ideas of sin, forgiveness, and repentance. Yes, the young girl, her mother, and the doctors who performed the procedure could go to confession, repent for their actions, be forgiven, and start receiving communion again. But did they really sin? And do people who have abortions really need to be forgiven? Those questions are rarely asked in the larger debates about what the end of *Roe v. Wade* will do to the Catholic Church in America. But they're also crucial to understanding why the case of the Brazilian girl offers us some clues about what may be coming next, not only for those seeking abortions in the United States but for all Christians in America too. And it raises uncomfortable questions about sin and forgiveness for the Catholic Church and the people who belong to it, and for the conservative Evangelicals who have also played a part in creating sweeping political changes that have robbed many women of agency over their bodies.

Five decades of relentless focus on abortion above all other issues, compounded with ongoing fallout from the clergy abuse crisis, has driven many Catholics out of the church, and younger Evangelicals are also beginning to follow. Widely cited statistics about the demographic decline of Christianity in America are so familiar to some of us who cover religion that we can recite them by memory at this point. For every person who joins the Catholic Church, six Catholics leave. There are now more ex-Catholics in America than practicing ones. Thirty percent of Southern Baptists reported in 2023 that they never attend church. And the end of legal abortion in America will likely mean even more attrition out of the church for the majority of Christians who believe abortion should stay legal and therefore safe.

The concern of many, both Catholic and not, is that the conservative Christian judges on the Supreme Court will use the ruling to end Roe to erode additional rights that protect bodily autonomy, like the rights to contraception and same-sex marriage. Technically, these things are also off-limits to Catholics and Evangelicals alike as both are considered sinful, and one would need to repent to be forgiven of them. But along with abortions, which Christian women have clearly been having for quite some time, contraception use and same-sex relationships are common among members of the church. The days of enormous Catholic families, which I frequently saw as a child, are long gone, belying the notion that American Catholics see contraceptive use, which Pope Pius XI once described as "stained by a great and mortal flaw," as a sinful act in need of forgiveness. And given that studies show a not insignificant number of Catholic priests are gay men trapped in the closet, the idea, too, that same-sex relationships are sinful makes the whole church seem to reek of hypocrisy.

The history of how the Catholic Church came to see abortion as a sin is long and complicated, but the debate has been consistently focused on two things: when life begins in the womb, and when the fetus achieves "ensoulment." The idea of ensoulment goes all the way back to Aristotle, who believed ensoulment occurred around the fortieth day of pregnancy for male fetuses and the ninetieth day for female ones (and we can note that misogynistic ancient Greek views of women have certainly left an imprint on many Christian churches today). That belief was passed on to St. Augustine—who himself abandoned a woman and the child of his she bore—and to St. Thomas Aquinas. The idea of delayed ensoulment persisted in church teaching until the nineteenth century, clouding the issue of when abortion was and wasn't permissible. When more sophisticated science about pregnancy entered the picture in the twentieth century, the church decided that ensoulment and life begin at the moment of conception. For some victims of sexual assault, this would turn out to have dire consequences.

***

The Catholic Church and American Evangelicals who relentlessly pressed for the end of Roe share something in common. They are both obsessed with the notion of sexual purity, and that obsession is laser-focused on the bodies of women. Before the Reformation, the Catholic Church deliberately created a cult of virginity around the body of Mary, the mother of Jesus. In spite of Gospel references to Jesus's siblings—the *adelphoi,* meaning "of the same womb"—the church has spent centuries doing logical acrobatics to keep Mary perpetually virginal. Jesus's brothers and sisters have become stepsiblings, cousins, or adopted family members. But as illogical as it might be, the idea of Mary's virginity seems to have stuck in the collective imagination. According to Pew Research, nearly all American Christians state they believe Jesus was born to a virgin mother.

Virginity itself has been the subject of obsessive debate in the church for centuries. Thomas Aquinas dedicates five articles of the *Summa Theologica* to the question of whether or not virginity is a virtue. He declares virginity "most excellent" because "it surpasses the chastity of both widowhood and marriage." In church teaching, chastity in marriage means monogamy, and in widowhood it means refraining from sex after the death of a spouse. In other words, a woman whose virginity is intact will always be better, purer, and more sanctified.

Aquinas further says that if a virgin is raped, she maintains her "aureole"—what we'd describe today as a halo, or an air of holiness—but only as long as she "retains unfailingly the purpose of perpetual virginity." In some cases, it was even believed that a virgin who was raped but forswore further sexual contact with men would miraculously regrow her hymen. Never mind that a hymen is not necessarily a sign of virginity and that it can be broken by anything from a tampon to gynecologist's speculum. It is on these understandings of virginity that Christian understandings of purity are built.

The Catholic Church has for centuries also created a cult around the idea of "virgin martyrs," who were usually young girls who were killed by their rapists. It's disturbing to most modern readers that many of these girls, who were children with little to no understanding of sex or biology, much less psychology, supposedly forgave the men who raped or tried to rape them. How does a child, who does not understand what sex is, forgive a person who has weaponized it against her? And even if some of these girls and women were old enough to understand what was happening, why does dying to protect their purity vault them onto the path toward sainthood? And how is this still happening today?

***

At 3 p.m. on July 5, 1902, Maria Goretti, an eleven-year-old Italian girl, was stabbed fourteen times by an orphaned man of twenty who lived with her impoverished farming family. Alessandro Serenelli had previously threatened Maria with rape, and on this day, he reportedly tried to strangle her when she refused him. According to one biography that heaves with pious prose, she shouted, "No, it is a sin! God does not want it!" Alessandro then repeatedly stabbed her with an awl, a sharpened spike usually used to puncture leather.

Maria survived long enough to be taken to the hospital. There, she is reported to have said she forgave Alessandro and wanted him in heaven with her. She died a day later. Serenelli was sentenced to thirty years in prison. When he was released, he reportedly went to Maria's mother and asked for forgiveness. He lived until 1970, and shortly before his death, he wrote a testimony that said, in part: "Maria Goretti, now a Saint, was my good Angel, sent to me through Providence to guide and save me. I still have impressed upon my heart her words of rebuke and of pardon. She prayed for me, she interceded for her murderer."

Fifty years after she died, Maria Goretti was declared a saint. In his homily at her canonization Mass, Pope Pius XII declared that Maria's sainthood was a model of sacrifice to protect her virginity. "There is then in this world, apparently turned upside down and immersed in hedonism not just a thin rank of settled elect of Heaven and the pure air, but a throng, immense multitudes on whom the supernatural perfume of Christian purity exerts an irresistible and promising fascination: promising yes, and reassuring.

In the martyrdom of Maria Goretti purity shone." Half a million people poured into St. Peter's Square for her canonization.

In 2015, Maria Goretti's body toured the United States. The website listing the dates when her relics would be viewable describes her as the "Patroness of Purity" whose greatest virtue was "her unyielding forgiveness of her attacker even in the midst of horrendous physical suffering." What that suffering led to was the conversion of her rapist, who later became a Capuchin Franciscan. That, in the eyes of the Vatican, was Maria's miracle: that a man was saved by trying to rape and kill a child.

Maria Goretti's story feels, for lack of a better word, medieval. The notion of dying for purity seems to be something from the distant past rather than the twentieth century, the kind of gory story portrayed in religious paintings tucked into the dim corners of chilly, crumbling churches in Europe. In *Commonweal Magazine*, B. D. McClay writes that "perhaps it is significant that Maria is not only a child, but a girl; one level removed from a boy, two levels removed from an adult male victim. Men are victims of sexual assault, too, but in terms of saints, it's the Marias who do the lifting for both genders." The miracle of Maria Goretti's supposed forgiveness was not hers to keep. It belonged to the man who killed her, the men who raised her up to sainthood, and the men who send her relics on tours of the world to encourage other victims of horrific violence to be just as forgiving. Even in death, Maria Goretti's forgiving body does not belong to her. It belongs to men.

The argument can be made that Maria Goretti's story might not be received the same way today. After all, when she was canonized in the mid-twentieth century, the age of consent in some American states and around the world ranged from ten or eleven years old to the teens. If Maria Goretti was eleven or twelve when her attempted rape and death happened, in some parts of the world, she was nearly old enough to be married. In 1959, Elvis Presley, who was twenty-five, would start dating his wife, Priscilla, who was fourteen. In 1994, R&B singer Aaliyah's age was changed from fifteen to eighteen on the marriage certificate so she could be married to twenty-seven-year-old R. Kelly, who was later convicted of sex trafficking multiple minors, as well as physically abusing women. During Kelly's 2022 trial, one victim, named only as Faith, said to Kelly, "I hope you forgive yourself. I forgive myself." According to reporters, Kelly would not even look her in the eye.

It might be conceptually challenging to connect Maria Goretti to the victims of a contemporary R&B singer. But somehow, their stories exist in the same century. Maria Goretti was canonized less than twenty years before R. Kelly was born. And ideas of women and girls dying and suffering to protect themselves from rape and still somehow being forgiving models of purity and chastity still persist today. In 2018, in the thick of the #MeToo movement that exposed untold numbers of sexual assaults and cases of sexual harassment, Pope Francis put a new "virgin martyr" named Anna Kolesárová on the path toward sainthood by beatifying her. This little-known teenage girl will someday become a saint because a man tried to rape her, and because she died praying, she supposedly forgave him.

Kolesárová died during an attempted rape in Slovakia in 1944, when a Russian soldier shot her. Even today, the Vatican calls this a death "in defensum casitatis," or to protect her virginity. At the beatification Mass in 2018—the same year sexual abuse victims advocacy group Time's Up called for a deeper investigation into R. Kelly—Slovakian Cardinal Becciu said Kolesárová "was killed for her resistance and firmness in defending her physical integrity and the virtue of chastity." Like Maria Goretti, he continued, she "defended her virginity with martyrdom." The Slovak bishops further said Kolesárová should be a model for the youth of today dealing with "temptations against purity." But is a teenage girl being threatened with forced sex at gunpoint really resisting "temptation"? In the case of Maria Goretti, is an eleven-year-old who is about to be stabbed really able to forgive the man who is about to sexually assault her if she doesn't have a clear understanding of sex or rape?

These questions of bodily autonomy and forgiveness range beyond the Catholic Church and into every social realm, including politics, art, culture, and education. Abuse victims, from the hundreds of gymnasts assaulted by Larry Nassar to Monica Lewinsky to Harvey Weinstein's victims, have reframed the narrative of what happens when a powerful man takes advantage of a woman who is under his control, trying to get people to understand that everything from language to rape can be sexual abuse. In religion, this is further complicated by the inherent power of pastors, priests, theologians, and other men who exercise both emotional and spiritual control over adults and children. Because "good"

Christians are supposed to forgive, that means Christian victims of sexual abuse are under tremendous pressure to forgive their abusers, even when those abusers are their fellow Christians.

Rachel Denhollander was the first woman to come forward and publicly accuse former USA gymnastics coach Larry Nassar of sexual abuse. Eventually, more than two hundred women would come forward and reveal Nassar groomed and molested them when they were as young as six years old. Denhollander, who has also spoken up about abuse in church settings, is also an Evangelical Christian. Nassar himself was a practicing Catholic, a eucharistic minister at his church, and a catechist who taught classes on the Catholic faith to children. In her 2018 victim impact statement about Nassar, Denhollander's forgiveness of Nassar made headlines and went viral. But, as she told *Christianity Today*, this was an over-simplification of what she really told Nassar about forgiveness.

Denhollander's essay for *Christianity Today* is entitled "My Larry Nassar Statement Went Viral, but There's More to the Gospel than Forgiveness." In it, Denhollander says, Christians assume that "if the victim just forgives, all of the feelings are going to go away," and she adds that the media rushed to headlines that she had forgiven Nassar. However, according to Denhollander, "Very few, if any of them, have recognized what else came with that statement, which was a swift and intentional pursuit of God's justice." In her victim impact statement, Denhollander also actively problematizes this easy picture of forgiveness by stating that she hopes God will forgive Nassar some day because he needs God's forgiveness more than hers. The rest of the statement is focused on Nassar's actions, which she describes as "evil and wicked." She speaks of the horror felt in the courtroom and she pleas for a maximum sentence. When Christian media glossed over this part of her statement and seized instead on a message of forgiveness, they created a distortion of not only her words but the similar statements given by other victims of Nassar.

Denhollander says that what people forget when they talk about sexual assault and forgiveness is that it doesn't necessarily mean that being forgiving is the end of a victim's suffering. "The suffering here on earth is very real," she told *Christianity Today*, "and it does not go away simply because you forgive and release bitterness." She emphasized that Nassar's victims would continue to feel the implications of the assault for the rest of their lives, no matter how much the media might focus on the idea that they had "forgiven" him. Simone Biles, another gymnast assaulted by Nassar, confirmed this when she gave a statement before a Senate Judiciary Committee investigating the FBI's failure to respond to Nassar's abuse in 2021. Biles told the Senate that training for the 2020 Olympics had forced her to "live daily among the remainders of this story." Biles further said that she is still processing and recovering from the trauma of Nassar's abuse. She told the Senate, "I can assure you that the impacts of this man's abuse are not ever over or forgotten."

For Denhollander, Biles, and other women who were victimized by Nassar, forgiveness cannot be separated from the idea of accountability and justice. Nassar was sentenced to 175 years in prison. That is justice. But Denhollander says that forgiving him "does not mean that I minimize or mitigate or excuse what he has done." Instead, she feels it is about releasing bitterness and letting go of a personal desire for vengeance. There is nothing simple or sentimental about this version of forgiveness. It is, instead, a process, one that has no finite timeline.

But when Nassar himself asked for forgiveness, Judge Rosmarie Aquilina dismissed his apology to the victims as insincere. Nassar said to the abuse victims that he would "carry [their] words with [him] for the rest of [his] life," but the judge then read a previous letter Nassar sent her that said he was a good doctor and that he had been manipulated into pleading guilty. In one psychological study on forgiveness, a perpetrator making amends means "accepting responsibility for an act of betrayal, and offering genuine atonement for actions." Forgiveness was less likely to be granted when offenses were intentional. This would describe Nassar's actions, which were not only intentional but systematic. In the study, forgiveness was more likely to be granted when an act is unintentional, which made Nassar's apology even more insincere. Because he acted strategically and methodically, fooling the girls' parents and coaches into letting him have private access to them, it is much less likely these women would ever be able to forgive him. This makes Denhollander's statement about forgiveness even more remarkable. But, again, it was distorted and misunderstood.

Denhollander also states that forgiveness comes at a cost. She severed ties with her church and lost many Evangelical friends when she came forward about Nassar and about abuse accusations in her childhood church, Sovereign Grace Churches. She still speaks in the language of Evangelicalism, however, when she talks about the idea of obedience to the gospels. But as a spokesperson for many Christian victims of sexual assault, Denhollander's idea of gospel obedience isn't pious or sentimental. For her, obedience to the gospel and gospel forgiveness is about holding people accountable.

"Obedience," she told *Christianity Today*, "means that you pursue justice and you stand up for the oppressed and you stand up for the victimized, and you tell the truth about the evil of sexual assault and the evil of covering it up."

R. Kelly's victim who said she hopes he can forgive himself likely believes that doing so might help Kelly to turn his life around, to be a better person, to feel regret for decades of abuse of women and children. And, like Denhollander, she was willing to stand up and say that to the person who destroyed her life in court. But when Kelly was sentenced to thirty years in prison, he offered no apology and gave no sign of remorse. He was unrepentant, and so were many of the men who violated the women and children the Catholic Church venerates as martyrs for purity. But even this notion of dying for purity as a sign of forgiveness is full of contradictions. As Molly O'Reilly writes about Anna Kolesárová, "was she martyred because she heroically resisted 'temptation'? Or was she murdered by a man who tried to rape her at gunpoint? It can't be both."

***

In her essay "Defanging the Beast," about the Mennonite response to pastor and theologian John Yoder's decades of sexual abuse, Rachel Walter Goosen says that in Christian settings, sexual abuse is rampant because pressure on victims to be forgiving protects powerful church leaders like Yoder. According to sociologist Anson Shupe, "the moral weight of religious traditions often renders believers vulnerable to leaders' abuses." Believers expect the best, not the worst, from church leaders, which can lead to the kind of "circle the wagons" mentality that has protected abusive clergy for centuries. It can also lead to what we now refer to as "victim blaming," where the abused person is punished for coming forward and revealing the abuse.

Mennonites, a denomination that emerged from the Reformation, are among a number of churches that fall under the Anabaptist denominations. Quakers and Amish are probably better-known denominations in America, but Mennonites, who mostly migrated from Germany, have lived in America since the 1600s. Mennonites are also pacifists and will not join the military or participate in warfare. Like other Anabaptist groups, Mennonites place a high value on community above all else and practice disciplinary measures when someone acts in a way that might harm the community. The end goal of those measures is to reconcile the individual with the Mennonite community. Sometimes, this comes at a cost.

Yoder, whose influence went far beyond the Mennonite community through his highly regarded books on Christian pacifism and his position on the faculty at Notre Dame, abused at least one hundred women, according to a Mennonite accountability and discipline process that took place in the 1990s. Yoder went through seven rounds of discipline with Mennonite boards and covenant groups that attempted to counsel him rather than having him arrested or expelled. Mennonite pastor and writer Melissa Florer-Bixler writes in her book *How to Have an Enemy* that this attempt to "redeem" a sinner can have dire consequences for victims of abuse. Florer-Bixler says that "the attempt to resolve conflict with interpersonal strategies like empathy often disregards how coercion and force shape the lives of enemies." If Yoder's Mennonite brethren had been willing to see him as an enemy or a problem rather than focusing so much on forgiveness and reconciliation, they might have saved dozens of women from the abuse he doled out.

The amazing thing is, throughout the Mennonite reconciliation process, Yoder never seems to have apologized to the victims personally. The process was about reconciling Yoder to the community, not about the harm done to the women. B. D. McClay writes that the women Yoder abused "were both individually and collectively unimportant to Mennonite leadership, and if they became lost sheep, it was, in this view, by their own choice." Carolyn Holderread Heggen, one of the complainants against Yoder, said he told her that he "was sorry that we had misunderstood his intentions." Because Yoder stopped short of rape and because his reputation was so towering, Mennonites downplayed the abuse and spent years trying to reconcile Yoder into the community. At one point in the reconciliation process, it was proposed that Yoder write letters to each of the women he abused, offering forgiveness. This never happened.

Nonetheless, Yoder emerged from the controversy "a hero of repentance," according to Mark Oppenheimer in the *New York Times*. Yoder was welcomed back to worship at Prairie Street

Mennonite Church and died at age seventy, capping "a perfect narrative of redemption," and he was supported to the end by Mennonite leaders who "rehabilitated" him, even after his death. Nelson Kraybill, the president of the Anabaptist Mennonite Biblical Seminary, told the *South Bend Tribune* that after Yoder's death, "I would regret if his personal failures, which John Yoder acknowledged, were more widely publicized than the process of restoration and forgiveness." And at the end of Yoder's disciplinary process, ethicists Stanley Hauwerwas and Glen Stassen praised the Mennonite officials who worked to keep Yoder in the church because "churches have a tremendous need for his gifts."

About the women Yoder abused, there is much less information. Did they forgive him, even though he never quite asked them to? While I found dozens of articles about Yoder, I found far fewer from the women who he abused. This silencing is both deliberate and circumstantial. Many of the women stayed anonymous out of fear or shame and to protect the Mennonite community. But obviously, this urge to silence or shun victims for the sake of the institution while also pressuring them to be forgiving and understanding isn't uniquely a Mennonite issue. The Catholic theologian Andrew Greely wrote that for powerful men in church settings, "you can exploit, and your colleagues will protect you from the effects of your exploitation either by denying it or finding you another place to exercise your power."

In 2015, the Anabaptist Mennonite Biblical Seminary, where Yoder had taught and abused women for decades, held a service of "reunion, listening and confessing" for Yoder's victims. At that service, Martha Smith Good read "A Psalm of Lament for Abused Women," a "corporate lament" for multiple victims of Yoder's abuse. The lament included these lines:

> God of mercy, hear my plea.
> I am being destroyed.
> I feel abandoned and lonely.
> There is no safety; no one to protect me.
> There is no one to entrust with my secret.
>
> My abuser speaks eloquently of peace and justice,
> While I weep angry tears of betrayal.
> He walks the halls with confidence,
> While I am fearful of being seen.

***

Sexual abuse exists on a continuum. John Howard Yoder may not have raped most of the women he abused, but nonetheless, he changed their lives forever. Mentally, physically, and spiritually, they carry traumatic memories, ones that are not easily shed, particularly if they hope to remain part of their religious community. Rape, of course, can have one specifically difficult consequence for its victims, which is unintended pregnancy. In the pro-life movement, a woman choosing to forgive her rapist also chooses "life" if she chooses not to end the pregnancy as part of that forgiveness.

But this does not change the fact that the child, too, is a victim of rape. The child will forever have to live with the knowledge that their life began in violence, with a lack of consent. This is why many women who are raped, like the Rwandan woman Heather King holds up as an exemplary model of forgiveness, choose not to tell their children about the circumstances of their conception. They are trying to protect the child. Is that forgiveness? If the woman chooses for that child to live, the child deserves life. But what if she doesn't choose this? If a woman who has been raped, or has been the victim of incest, or finds herself unintentionally impregnated for any variety of reasons, some of which might bring an end to her life, goes out and seeks an abortion, does she need to be forgiven? What about the religious institution that would prevent that woman from procuring an abortion? If she dies as the result of a self-administered abortion, or if she descends into poverty or addiction as the result of bearing the child and the church that promised to be there for her doesn't help her, should she forgive it?

This presents an especially difficult question for Catholics, who are considered to be excommunicated if they have an abortion, even if it happens because of a rape. Because the Catholic Church considers abortion at any stage of pregnancy an act of murder, Catholics are taught to believe that every moment of conception will lead to a viable life, even though a zygote and a twenty-four-week-old fetus that can breathe on its own are not the same thing. The church currently states that life beginning at conception is a "scientific fact," but this, too, is debatable. Even with our more developed contemporary understanding of biology and embryology, scientists, ethicists, politicians, and theologians cannot agree when "personhood" begins. We know that not every fertilized egg implants, that miscarriages are common in the first part of pregnancy, and that in the vast majority of cases, people seek out abortions in the earliest stages of pregnancy. We also know that sometimes people need abortions in order to survive sepsis, cancer, and other things that can kill. So we have to ask, yet again: Why is abortion considered so terrible a sin that it incurs excommunication every time it happens?

Another irony to consider is that while abortion is considered an offense worthy of excommunication, rape is not. The man who attempted to rape Maria Goretti was forgiven and is even held up as an exemplar of repentance. The Catechism of the Catholic Church does describe rape as "evil," but it does not go so far as to say that a rapist should be excommunicated. So the narrative Heather King creates of the Rwandan woman "forgiving" her rapist essentially creates an idea that she "escaped" the mortal sin of abortion.

The church teaching on this is convoluted. In order for a person to incur excommunication, Canon Law 1323 states they must be over the age of sixteen, aware of the punishment for their sin, and free from "grave fear." Many real-world examples of abortion fall outside of those parameters. I attended Catholic schools for most of my elementary school years and went to a Catholic college, and while we were told that abortion was sinful, excommunication was never mentioned. But abortion was also not the central focus of the Catholic social teaching I encountered in my youth. The death penalty, humanitarian crises around the world, nuclear threat, and the racism pervasive in our local community were usually treated as more urgent issues.

In the decades since Roe became law, however, the Catholic Church in America has shifted its focus from issues of poverty, war, the death penalty, and the environment to eradicating abortion as its highest priority issue. Although beliefs about the legality of abortion are decidedly mixed among lay Catholics, the US Conference of Catholic Bishops' relentless focus on ending Roe has led to what the Catholic writer Garry Wills calls "the cult of the fetus," in which the life of the unborn trumps the life of the mother every time. The bishops have long sponsored events like the annual March for Life in DC and have formed generations of priests in seminaries who see abortion as the church's primary issue. And there's no mistaking the fact that this campaign has primarily targeted Catholic women. Just before the Supreme Court overturned Roe, San Francisco archbishop Salvatore Cordileone excommunicated Catholic former speaker of the house Nancy Pelosi for her support of abortion rights, ostensibly to encourage her to "repent." Pope Francis, meanwhile, has strongly advised that the eucharist should not be weaponized and used as a political tool. But the American bishops seem to have missed that message.

In an attempt to ease the pain of excommunication, in 2016, Pope Francis changed the manner in which excommunications are lifted for those who've had an abortion. In the past, a person seeking absolution for abortion would have to go to the bishop to get their excommunication lifted and to be absolved. Today, one can instead go straight to any parish priest. Unfortunately, however, most Catholics do not know about this change or the steps one can take to remain in the church after having an abortion because the church has barely broadcast this decision. Case in point: I was in Rome during the Jubilee Year of Mercy following Francis's decree, and this issue of easing excommunication for those who have had an abortion was never mentioned in the seminar I attended for journalists covering the church. And even with this change, there is still no guarantee that if you go to confession the priest will absolve you.

Technically, in the eyes of the church, anyone involved in an abortion needs to seek repentance, as in the case of the Brazilian girl's mother and doctors. But rarely do we hear of men involved in abortions doing this. The face of the anti-abortion movement is typically not a man but a woman, and not the low-income mother who is statistically the most likely person to seek one out. And you don't have to go far in Catholic whisper networks to hear of seminarians who impregnated girlfriends and procured abortions for them before going on to be ordained, priests doing the same, or the spotty history of popes with a series of mistresses who more than likely sought out some "assistance" from a local herbalist when one of those mistresses got into trouble.

Catholics and Evangelicals who are now arguing that the church will be there to support pregnant women seem to have forgotten that churches had fifty years since the legalization of Roe to build networks of community support, to lobby for family aid, and to provide viable alternatives for the babies they're so enthusiastic about welcoming. But in those fifty years, it has not done those things to a degree in any way adequate to the number of children who will be born into lives of violence, poverty, and hunger, or the number of women who will get sick and die from a lack of abortion access. To truly be "pro-life" and "pro family," the church could spend more money, provide more resources, and lobby harder for the lives of families. It does not, however, do these things to a degree that makes a demonstrable difference now, nor does it have concrete plans for the future, and millions of Americans are aware of this. So who is the real sinner here?

The fall of Roe and the celebratory nature of many Christian responses to it may mean more Americans will finally leave the church. This happened in Brazil, where the number of Catholics was already declining when the nine-year-old was excommunicated, and many more have left since. In Ireland, another historically Catholic country, the death of a woman whose demise came as the result of being turned away from an abortion to end her sepsis in 2012 created an international outcry. Ireland's own clergy abuse crisis, which involved tens of thousands of "illegitimate" children being abused in industrial schools and even more "fallen women" sent to work in asylums that still operated into the 1990s, caused more and more Irish people to shake off the Catholic Church's grip on their bodies and minds. In 2018, Ireland voted to make abortion legal.

When it comes to sin and forgiveness, the church tends to gloss over its own teaching on conscience. In *Gaudium et Spes*, one of the documents that came out of Vatican II, the church teaches Catholics that "[a person] has in [their] heart a law written by God," and that obeying our conscience is the thing from which our dignity arises. A person can seek out an abortion for a million reasons, but in each case, the decision as to whether or not it is a sin in need of forgiveness will happen in their conscience, not in the confessional, not in the chancery office, and not in the echoing hallways of the Vatican. For many in the coming weeks, months, and years who will see the death and suffering wrought by the end of Roe, that same conscience may well lead them away from the church that brought about that end. And they will probably never forgive it.

8

Just Let It Go

Why Self-Forgiveness Isn't Always Possible,
and How It Can Lead to Abuse

The apostle Paul told the Corinthians that a person who causes pain hurts not just one person but the whole community. "For such a one," he wrote, "this punishment by the majority is enough, so you should rather turn to forgive and comfort him." The purpose of this forgiveness, Paul goes on to say, is to outwit Satan, who desires division. As one contemporary pastor said about this passage, "When you choose not to forgive, you are choosing to welcome the demonic into your life."

The pastor who wrote this was Mark Driscoll. Driscoll, who in 1996 founded the megachurch Mars Hill in Seattle, was known for his aggressive, "bad boy" preaching style. He railed against women who wouldn't sexually submit to their husbands and frequently talked about the importance of masculinity in his sermons, which were broadcast online to audiences of hundreds of thousands. Behind the scenes, however, Driscoll's approach was closer to bullying and spiritual abuse. Using the online pseudonym "William Wallace," the hero of the movie Braveheart, Driscoll had written discussion board posts referring to America as a "pussified nation" and called feminism "the enemy of every woman, every man, and God almighty." This kind of thinking was demonstrated in his behavior both in the pulpit and offstage.

Driscoll's rhetoric was just the tip of the iceberg, however, and by 2014, twenty-one former Mars Hill pastors filed a complaint asking for Driscoll to be removed. Driscoll was known to scream, shout, threaten to "destroy" former staff members, and shun people who upset him, severing them from the Mars Hill community. He was able to get away with this because the church was enormously successful, making a lot of money from its huge congregation and from Driscoll's book sales. In his apology letter to the church, Driscoll didn't apologize to any individuals but to the church as an institution, promising he'd post less on social media and take on fewer speaking engagements because his "angry young prophet days were over" and it was time for him to become "a helpful, Bible-teaching father." Driscoll, in other words, had already forgiven himself and was ready to move on. After enormous public pressure, he finally resigned from Mars Hill and went on to found a new church in Phoenix in 2016, where by many accounts his bullying and abusive behavior continue in the form of shunning, verbal abuse, threats, and distrust.

If Mark Driscoll has forgiven himself, it's not particularly surprising. In some ways, the argument to forgive yourself makes sense. It's a running theme in popular psychology that the person who cannot forgive themselves for making a mistake or hurting another person will never be able to move forward with their life and will remain trapped in a cycle of self-doubt or a loop of making the same mistakes and hurting the same people. Perhaps this is true, and psychologists and theologians have certainly written plenty about this notion.

But forgiving yourself in the sense of making amends with yourself, trying to do better by yourself, and coming to an understanding about yourself? This is not as simple as "forgive yourself" or "just let it go" might seem. For people with mental health issues, especially people with clinical depression, decades of therapy, medication, and self-reflection sometimes aren't enough for them to achieve the peace with themselves and their pasts that advocates of universal forgiveness promise. For people in recovery from addiction, the focus is on understanding powerlessness over an addiction, and while the twelve-step model emphasizes conducting a "fearless moral inventory of ourselves," the notion of self-forgiveness is not etched into the process. Offering amends to others is, instead, more important.

Always falling back on "forgive yourself" can also contribute to a lack of self-accountability. Obviously, not every person is a sociopath or narcissist using self-forgiveness as a tool for ignoring other people's feelings. Many people who advocate for self-forgiveness have struggled to arrive at it themselves, and self-forgiveness can be beneficial for helping some people to break patterns and hold themselves accountable. But too much emphasis on self-forgiveness can lead to abusers letting themselves off the hook. It can cause people to move forward from trauma without understanding trauma's impact on their bodies and minds. And it can also lead us to be too forgiving of other people who might do us harm.

The psychologist Matt James writes that because we think of our lives as a continuum, when we try to forgive ourselves for something from the past, we're essentially "trying to release something that feels as if it's part of us." Because our pasts define who we are, it can feel easier to forgive someone else than it can to forgive ourselves. Doing so would also mean we're releasing some essential part of our life narratives. But in order to be self-forgiving, we also have to acknowledge our flaws. For some people with inflated self-esteem, that alone is impossible.

In many cases, people who abuse and find it easy to forgive themselves exhibit traits of narcissism or sociopathy. Narcissism, which the *Diagnostic and Statistic Manual of Mental Disorders* describes as including "grandiosity, need for admiration, and a lack of empathy," can clearly be seen in many cases of abuse. This personality type would make it easier for someone to self-forgive since they may struggle to understand that they've done something wrong in the first place. Sociopaths, who "habitually and pervasively disregard or violate the rights and considerations of others without remorse," might also find it easy to forgive themselves because the disorder can cause a pattern of irresponsible behavior and a tendency to behave impulsively, which could mean they are prone to let themselves off the hook.

For people with low self-esteem, however, flaws are all they can see. Peg O'Connor, who teaches philosophy and gender studies, refers to this as a form of self-deception. She writes that these people can't forgive themselves because they suffer from exceptionalism, when "you maintain a standard for yourself that is far higher than the one you use for others." This is naturally a cousin to perfectionism, which can also hold a person back from self-forgiveness. O'Connor goes on to say that exceptionalism can become a form of confirmation bias. "Every act confirms your inadequacy or culpability, which exacerbates shame," she writes. "You believe everything you do and everything about you is bad or wrong or hurtful, and this reinforces your view that someone like you doesn't deserve forgiveness."

O'Connor compares this state of mind to an abused spouse who finally leaves the relationship. When she can't forgive herself, it's because she needs to acknowledge both why she stayed in that relationship and why she left it. She has to be able to see that "she did the best she could in a difficult situation" rather than feeling that she failed by ceding control to an abusive partner. But to get there, she has to learn to value and respect herself. This is a difficult battle for someone who has been abused. When a person is constantly being denigrated and disrespected, their internal monologue turns into one where they constantly focus on self-denigration and self-disrespect. They can also get caught up in an internalized shame spiral.

Shame is a behavioral mitigator. The writer Anneli Rufus says that shame "is fear of rejection, humiliation, unacceptability, of being bad in a good world." Left unchecked, according to Rufus, shame can lead to regret, guilt, self-loathing, and fear. Narcissists and sociopaths are often described as being incapable of shame, and a lack of shame could also mean that unlike the people they hurt, they can easily move to self-forgiveness. But shame is part and parcel of how we talk about sin in religion, even when this shame is misdirected, as it is for victims of abuse. For all of religion's focus on insisting that people forgive one another, the tangled threads of internalized shame can mean that religious people may be good at granting forgiveness to others, but they struggle to do the same for themselves.

***

Jesus never tells us, "Just forgive yourself." We don't even know if he would have understood that as a concept, since much of our understanding of the interior life of the mind comes from psychology, a twentieth-century lens that doesn't always work when applied to a two-thousand-year-old text. In the past, people may have forgiven themselves, but they didn't seem to dwell on it or tell others to do it with the same frequency that happens today. Many of what Christians now see as penitential practices that theoretically might help them arrive at self-forgiveness didn't exist in Jesus's imagination. Ash Wednesday marks the beginning of Lent every year, but Jesus didn't participate in either of those and in fact warned people not to walk around showing off how penitent they could be. Religionists in his day didn't go to confession or say a Confetior during Mass, telling God that they sinned "through what I have done, and what I have failed to do."

Instead, Jesus would have participated in Yom Kippur, one of the two *yanim noraim*, or Days of Awe, in the Jewish High Holy Days. Yom Kippur is described in Leviticus as the day when "atonement shall be made for you, to purify you" (Lev 16:30). While rituals and sacrifices were practiced in Jewish temples year-round, biblical scholar Candida Moss describes Yom Kippur as "something like a religious deep clean," an opportunity for Jewish people to use atonement to God and to others to eliminate their sins. For Christians, there is an echo of this notion on Ash Wednesday, when foreheads are marked with a cross and they're reminded "you are dust, and to dust you shall return," after which they enter into the penitential season of Lent. Repent and atone, Yom Kippur and Lent remind us, because you don't know the day or the hour. But as a Jew, Jesus would have understood forgiveness as something owed to other people. Yom Kippur's prayers are about making amends to people you've harmed, not to yourself.

There is a difference between atoning to others, repenting for harm done to others, and repenting to ourselves. Making amends to other people is actionable. You can see and feel the difference it makes when you wipe away a debt or help someone move past harm you've done to them. Making amends to yourself is much more abstract. Much of our self-forgiveness talk is about letting go of shame over things we've done and said. And if religion itself is the thing that feeds the internalized shame that prevents a person from forgiving themselves, this is much more complicated than "just let it go."

***

Just like deciding to stay in a church means trying to understand what forgiveness really means, negotiating the decision to leave can also be an interior journey through new ideas about self-forgiveness. In the past few years, it's been pretty much impossible to go on social media if you run in religion writing circles without running into a Christian, usually a former Evangelical, who is "deconstructing." The term, which originates in literary theory, was originally used by Jaques Derrida to describe the idea that in language, meaning is not fixed or static but subject to multiple interpretations. Those interpretations will be guided by the desire of the reader. In other words, a feminist will read Jane Austen differently, as the story of women claiming their own agency in relationships, from someone who thinks Austen writes simple little love stories.

It's unclear exactly when Christians started using the term "deconstruction" to talk about interrogating their beliefs, but it's been heard in post-Evangelical circles for at least a decade, if not longer. The writer Blake Chastain, who had himself grown up Evangelical, first used the hashtag #exvangelical in 2016, looking to create "a safe space for people going through similar experiences." Chastain's hashtag led to a podcast, an online community, and a book he's writing. All of these were attempts to help deconstructing Christians find a way to square their post-Evangelical lives with their former beliefs, which often focused on harsh judgments of women, queer people, and liberals. Chrissy Stroop, a journalist and academic, soon followed with #emptythepews, which she also turned into a book of the same name, an anthology of essays by former Evangelicals. Stroop is also a transgender woman, lending another layer to her advocacy for people harmed by Evangelicalism's often harsh teachings on gender.

Deconstructing mostly focuses on people unpacking what they were taught and how "high-control" religious denominations have impacted them, but, by necessity, it also sometimes veers into the language of self-forgiveness. If a former Christian has been part of a religious denomination that asked them to check their identity at the door, clawing back the person they were really can involve letting go of many layers of shame and trauma. In 2018, as the deconstruction conversation was beginning to attract the interest of academics, the sociologist Andrea Nica wrote in *Religion Dispatches* that "leaving fundamentalist, strict religions can have negative health consequences, both perceived and actual, that manifest in the body and mind. Research shows that individuals who come out to family members, specifically as an atheist . . . report that families often react with anger and rejection, as communication deteriorates, and distrust grows."

But what does deconstructing from religion have to do with self-forgiveness? For people who participated in strict religious denominations, which could include anything from Jehovah's Witnesses to FLDS Mormons, from traditionalist Catholics to Shi'ite Muslims or Hasidic Jews or even Zen Buddhists, the mindset they have been trained to have is one of suspicion and fear of outsiders. As a result, people who leave strict religious beliefs behind must reckon with the ways that their former beliefs led them to do damage to other people.

Tara Westover was raised by Mormon survivalist parents who didn't believe in vaccines or public schools and were so suspicious of the federal government that Westover didn't have a birth certificate until she was nine years old. Westover wrote in her memoir *Educated* that as a fundamentalist Mormon, "my life was narrated for me by others. Their voices were forceful, emphatic, absolute." Even after she left home to attend Brigham Young University, her parents' religious teachings and paranoid worldview, along with physical and psychological abuse by her brother, had so impacted Westover's mental health that a professor recommended she leave the USA to do graduate work to put as much distance between herself and her family as possible.

In an interview with *Deseret News*, a mainstream Mormon news service, Westover said that part of why she wrote *Educated*, which became a massive bestseller, was to get people to think differently about forgiveness. In her parents' understanding, Westover says, the purpose of forgiveness was always reconciliation. Her parents' religion, she said, "made it seem like reconciliation was the highest form of forgiveness and I just didn't know whether I would ever be able to reconcile with my family, so I wanted to tell a story that would be about forgiveness but wouldn't necessarily be about reconciliation." This depiction of forgiveness without reconciliation was part of the enthusiastic response to Westover's book. It gave many readers who were themselves separating from their family's religious beliefs permission to believe that "you can miss a person every day, and still be glad that they are not in your life," as she writes in *Educated*.

In many ways, *Educated* is also a story of self-forgiveness. Westover's narrative arc of going from homeschooled Mormon fundamentalist to Cambridge PhD is radically strange and wildly exceptional, so that, too, is a major part of her book's appeal. But throughout the book, there is also a thread of Westover steadily unraveling her identity from her family's beliefs to re-create herself as an entirely new person. To get there, like many other people who've moved past fundamentalist beliefs, she may not need to reconcile with her family, but she has to reconcile with herself and try to understand why she believed what they believed and how she moved past this. It's an inspirational story, which is also part of its appeal.

But not everyone is able to forgive themselves for participating in religious denominations that do damage in the name of God. There is a running joke among practicing, lapsed and former Catholics alike that we suffer from "Catholic guilt." This usually refers to feeling guilty for indulging in something pleasurable, usually referring to sex, but also extending to anything the church frowns upon, from something as significant as abortion to something as insignificant as eating chocolate during Lent. But after years of writing about and interviewing hundreds of practicing, lapsed, and former Catholics, I would argue that "Catholic guilt" also involves feeling ashamed or embarrassed about being part of the church when it does something damaging and extends to not being able to forgive yourself for being part of the church.

There's a reason many Catholics left the church during the abuse crisis. There's a reason many more will be likely to leave in the wake of the church's role in the end of *Roe v. Wade*. If Catholics are taught that sinfulness is both external and internal, both thought and deed, "what I have done and what I have failed to do," the sins of the institution are our sins as well. Every time a diocese or a religious order releases a list of clergy accused of abuse, Catholics have to brace themselves to see the name of a clergy member we trusted appearing on that list. People in the church I considered to be mentors and friends have been revealed as abusers, and while there was no way I would forgive them for being abusers, there were also times when I couldn't forgive myself for not being able to prevent their abuse.

In 2022, my byline appeared in a Catholic magazine next to the byline of a Catholic writer who was accused of abuse by multiple people who worked for a religious nonprofit he formerly operated. I'd denounced him publicly, but still struggle years later to forgive myself for not doing more. I could have requested my magazine editors not to work with him, but they are Catholic priests who believe that forgiveness always involves reconciliation. They very likely know his history, and they choose to work with him anyway. I could quit the magazine in protest, but then who would write the kinds of things I do about accountability in the church? I could post about my frustration and anger on social media, but that wouldn't take away the fact that this man still has enough clout to make these kinds of comebacks.

So, it is a struggle to forgive myself for being part of a religious institution that enables and even platforms destructive people like him, even while the same religious institution feeds my mind, soul, scholarly, and creative work. This is a bind that untold others likely find themselves in. Deconstruction and the ensuing journey to self-forgiveness can be a privilege because in some cases, it's impossible or not even desirable for a person to sever themselves from their faith.

Deconstruction reached absurdist heights in 2021 when former Evangelical Josh Harris released a $275 "deconstruction starter pack" course through his website. Harris, who wrote the 1996 Evangelical chastity guidebook *I Kissed Dating Goodbye*, was a celebrity of Christian purity culture. He led a megachurch and sold thousands of copies of his books, but his 2019 divorce led to his "questioning the things I built my life around," as he told *Newsweek* in 2021. Harris's website also included $1,750 group coaching sessions for "learning your brand voice," which led many skeptics on social media to decry his attempt to make deconstruction itself into his brand. Harris claimed that by offering the deconstruction starter pack, he was trying to "help people" because deconstruction can be lonely and "healing can be found in sharing our stories." Ultimately, Harris ended up pulling the deconstruction course, claiming the backlash had caused him to reconsider monetizing it, but the fact that only four people had paid to enroll may be the more telling reason.

It's clear that someone like Josh Harris has forgiven himself for the part he played in purity culture, which has been widely criticized both inside and outside of Christianity for pressuring people to marry young in order to have sex, which often ended up being bad and even abusive sex. Many people who experienced purity culture in the 80s and 90s have also talked about how tied up it was in misogynistic and homophobic ways of seeing the world and how it intensified the fear and suspicion of secularism.

Of course, many of the same white Evangelicals like Josh Harris who created the purity culture movement were among the voting base that elected Donald Trump; were part of the QAnon movement that led to the siege of the capitol on January 6, 2020; and fueled the anti-vaccination movement that exacerbated the COVID-19 pandemic. Do they forgive themselves? Do they even feel the guilt or shame that would lead a person to seek forgiveness? This, like so many other things about our country today, is unclear. But what is clear is that self-righteousness and greed might be enough to cause a person to believe they don't need to be forgiven in the first place because in their minds, they've done nothing wrong.

***

One side effect of being a religion writer is that I follow and am followed by a lot of members of the clergy on social media. Some of these people have become real, trusted friends; others are the kinds of acquaintances that online life leads us to interact with without really knowing one another, but I'd still usually describe most of them as people I like. The string of cases of spiritual and religious leaders being outed for abuse has been a way of separating the wheat from the chaff among the clergy I interact with on social media. When someone defends an abusive leader or denigrates abuse victims, it's easy to click "unfollow." I don't forgive those people, but it's also difficult to forgive myself for having interacted with them in friendly ways in the past.

In 2019, Jean Vanier, the charismatic founder and leader of the L'Arche community, died at the age of ninety. L'Arche is an international community with houses all over the world where people with intellectual disabilities live and work alongside people without intellectual disabilities. Unlike other homes for intellectually disabled people where they are often treated in patronizing or paternalistic ways, L'Arche focuses on mutuality and on building relationships. For his founding of L'Arche and nurturing it over decades, Vanier was described by many as a "living saint."

But if the sex abuse crisis has taught us anything, it's that we shouldn't declare people saints until long after their physical lives are over. Less than a year after Vanier's death, L'Arche International reported that six women had come forward to say Vanier had physically, emotionally, and spiritually abused them between 1970 and 2005. Vanier had a long-standing relationship with a Dominican priest named Thomas Phillipe, who cofounded L'Arche. Before he himself was accused of abuse, Vanier referred to Phillipe as his "spiritual father," but Phillipe had long been an abuser of women himself, claiming that sexual abuse of women led to "mystical experiences." Vanier would later use the same excuse for his own abuse. Both Phillipe and Vanier were obsessed with demanding secrecy from their victims as the L'Arche movement grew, along with their own reputations for holiness.

The reaction to the news of Vanier's abuse sent shockwaves not only through the Catholic world but through the many people who had admired the work of L'Arche. To the organization's credit, they immediately assigned an independent commission of experts from theology, psychology, sociology, and history to investigate the story of Phillipe's and Vanier's histories of abuse. That report was released in February of 2023. It's over eight hundred pages in length, and it tells a gruesome story of how "holy" and charismatic men can use forgiveness as a weapon against people they've abused and how self-forgiveness allows them to get away with it. It also provides some textbook examples of the reasons why abuse victims, whether they've been abused physically, emotionally, or spiritually, should not feel they owe these men any forgiveness.

According to the report, Phillipe was able to continuously abuse women because his provincial leaders in the Dominicans fell for his playing the role of a "repentant penitent" and had esteem for his work with the poor and disabled. Even before he and Vanier founded L'Arche, Phillipe had a pattern of acknowledging his abuse, asking for forgiveness for hurting his religious superiors, and insisting on a long penance. According to the report, however, Phillipe never mentioned his victims in these requests for forgiveness.

As for Vanier, a recollection in the report from a person who interviewed one of his abuse victims states that Vanier believed that sexually abusing women was "a good and acceptable way to relate" to them spiritually. This person goes on to say that "'one of the things' [the abuse victim] said to me 'that stays with me was he keeps asking [for] forgiveness, but he's never said he's sorry.'" It's easy to conclude from these accounts that Phillipe and Vanier had essentially forgiven themselves. Because Vanier didn't say he was sorry, and because Phillipe was only sorry for harming the reputation of the Dominican order, the victims of both men's abuse don't owe either of them any forgiveness. If it's not asked for, how can it be owed?

By all accounts in the report, Vanier remained in thrall to Phillipe even after Phillipe's death, and some people have gone so far as to say that L'Arche was essentially founded as a cult. In its analysis of the L'Arche investigation, *Sojourners* magazine reported that L'Arche began as a cover for the mystical sexual sect "Living Water," founded by Phillipe in the 1950s. According to *Sojourners'* Mitchell Atencio, "Vanier founded L'Arche as a cover to reunite a group who practiced contemplation and spiritual direction with nudity and sexual touch." This included "spiritual deviation, manipulation, incestuous representations of relationships between Jesus and Mary." Vanier continued to use his work with L'Arche as a screen for these behaviors for decades. L'Arche leaders were apparently "stunned" by this report. L'Arche was so highly regarded, and Vanier so beloved, that he had successfully been able to hide his abusive behavior for nearly half a century.

Many of my clergy friends in real life and on social media have lived in L'Arche communities, so it's not too surprising that in the immediate aftermath of the 2023 report being released, their reactions ranged from defensive to penitent. But the reaction of one person in particular took me aback. He was not going to read the report, he said, because L'Arche was such an important part of his vocation story. He felt that what people should do instead of reading the report would be to go and visit a L'Arche community or donate to one because the work of the community should outweigh the story of its very flawed founders.

But the argument about Vanier isn't that L'Arche doesn't do good work. It is that we have to stop forgiving abusive religious leaders and that we have to stop allowing them to forgive themselves. We also must stop ignoring the role abuse played in the founding of those organizations.

This propensity in churches to downplay the abuse of charismatic religious leaders because of the good work their organizations do is connected to the idea of self-forgiveness. In the 2021 podcast *The Turning*, women who'd left the Missionaries of Charity, Mother Teresa's religious order, recounted stories of only being able to visit their families once a decade, not being allowed to have private conversations, and being told to flagellate themselves on a regular basis to "mortify" their flesh and drive away physical desire. Mother Teresa was seen as so holy and so connected to God that the sometimes questionable ways she treated the sick people her order cared for, along with the sisters in her order, were often overlooked.

A British medical journal that visited one of Mother Teresa's care homes in the 1990s reported that medical care for the dying "was haphazard and that nursing sisters were required to take decisions for which they were not qualified . . . [and] that there was a lack of strong painkillers which he related to Mother Teresa's view that pain was a blessing." Canadian doctors who did a follow-up report in 2013, on the eve of her canonization, said that Mother Teresa was "anything but a saint."

Does this negate the work of the Missionaries of Charity altogether? No. But it should make us try to understand why Mother Teresa saw the things she asked of the sisters in her charge and the way her homes were run as acceptable. It's well reported that she herself underwent a multi-decade crisis of faith, what the Jesuit priest James Martin has called an "intense spiritual darkness." In that spiritual darkness, perhaps Mother Teresa was distracted enough not to see what was going on around her. Perhaps she was too focused on the idea of suffering as the way of Jesus. Perhaps she had forgiven herself for the shortcomings of her religious order because of the greater work that it did. We can't know her interior life, but we do know that if a person is called saintly and holy for most of their lives, that must impact their self-perception. And one of those impacts can be a propensity to forgive oneself. If others insist you're a saint, and saints teach us how to be forgiving, it's easy to imagine that a person's ego might override their ability to be self-perceptive to the point that they can "just move on," because that is what they usually do.

***

Just after the report on Jean Vanier was released, *Sojourners* began airing episodes of a podcast about Vanier they'd been working on for over a year. In the first episode, reporter Jenna Barnett visited a L'Arche community in the DC area. There, she met Charles, who's one of what L'Arche calls its "Core Members," the adults with disabilities who live in the homes. Charles was dressed as a Texas

Ranger in a cowboy hat and badge, and when Barnett asked him what he'd do if he was able to speak to Vanier, Charles said he'd tell Vanier, "You did a bad thing," and then he'd arrest him. As the conversation went on, however, Barnett talked further with Charles about how Vanier's abuse had hurt both the L'Arche communities and the women he abused. It's worth quoting a bit of their dialogue here, taken from the episode transcript.

> **Barnett:** If you could talk to the survivors, the women who he hurt, what would you wanna say to them?
>
> **Charles:** I'd say, uh, I'm very sorry this happened to you. God bless you. We'll help you get on your feet.
>
> **Barnett:** That's kind.
>
> **Charles:** I love those people that he hurt.
>
> **Barnett:** You love them?
>
> **Charles:** I love them, deeply.
>
> **Barnett:** Even though you've never met them?
>
> **Charles:** Right. Well maybe someday I will meet them.

It's remarkable to think about how Charles is able to be forgiving on behalf of Vanier, but also how his first instinct, and that of the L'Arche leadership, was to be quick to investigate how Vanier kept his secrets and to try and be accountable to the women who Vanier hurt. It is exceptional, but it shouldn't be. Instead of making those women feel guilty for holding Vanier's secrets, the leadership of L'Arche was willing to risk its reputation by swiftly moving into accountability. This is, unfortunately, rare for any institution. And perhaps instead of asking those women to try and forgive themselves for keeping Vanier's secret for so long, it's people from L'Arche like Charles who will do the forgiving instead.

I found another answer to this question self-forgiveness and accountability on Reddit, of all places. While Reddit can be chaotic and it brims over with conspiracy theories and memes, its mental health communities are full of helpful advice and support for people who often feel misunderstood by the medical community. In the Reddit sub for people with borderline personality disorder, which can cause severe mood swings and issues with impulsiveness and inappropriate anger, a person asked how to forgive themselves for being abusive in the past. Another user replied, "I can't, and don't forgive myself for past actions. I can't change them, and to forgive them does a disservice to the people I have hurt." They went on to say, "What I do is use the understanding of what I've done, the shame and pain from the damage I have done to fellow human beings to AGGRESSIVELY say 'never again.' I can't change what I've done, but I can change what I WILL do."

Not everyone arrives at this level of accountability or is able to say that forgiving themselves would be letting themselves off the hook. Even after a popular 2021 podcast called *The Rise and Fall of Mars Hill* exposed his abuse to thousands of listeners who'd never previously heard of him, Mark Driscoll is back on the Evangelical speaking circuit, and he has a new congregation at Trinity Church in Phoenix, Arizona. Its website cheerfully declares that "with Pastor Mark, it's all about Jesus!" Driscoll has clearly forgiven himself and moved on. A friend recently drove by his new church on a trip to Arizona. On a Sunday morning, its parking lot overflowed.

9

If Not Forgiveness, Then What?

Restorative Justice and the Messy Work of Atonement

A group of women sit on hay bales in a barn. They range from white-haired elders to girls twisting their hair into intertwined braids to young mothers with multiple children. Their sleeves are long, their skirts long, their hair covered by scarves. They are Mennonites. Most modern Mennonites dress, work, and socially integrate themselves like most other Christians, but some Mennonites live in separatist sects with strict discipline, little to no education for women, and a fundamentalist understanding of forgiveness. For them, either you grant forgiveness every time you're asked for it, or you go to hell.

This is a scene from *Women Talking*, a 2022 film based on a novel by Miriam Towes. The novel itself is loosely based on the true story of a Mennonite separatist colony in Bolivia, where over a hundred women and girls were drugged and raped by the colony's men. Sarah Polley, who directed and adapted the film's screenplay, has written about her own experiences of sexual assault and wrestling with the concept of forgiveness in her memoir *Run Toward the Danger*. Polley also told an audience at the New York Film Festival that she wanted to portray forgiveness in a nuanced way in the film. Forgiveness, she said, is something "we have to wield carefully because when harm is still being done, I think forgiveness can be misconstrued as permission."

That line, which Polley says came out of a collaborative conversation about forgiveness with the women in the cast, is paraphrased in the film. And the film never depicts these women forgiving the men who harmed them and their children. Instead, it shows us what it means when women learn to forgive one another for participating in a patriarchal system that enables abuse by forcing women to forgive. Greta, an older female character, apologizes to her daughter Autje for encouraging Autje to stay with an abusive husband. "You forgave him, as you were told to," Greta says. "What you were required to do was a misuse of forgiveness."

Throughout the film, as the women debate staying in the colony and forgiving the men as their Mennonite faith demands, or leaving and condemning themselves to excommunication and damnation, they wrestle with what it would mean to refuse to be forgiving. Ona, who is pregnant from a rape, asks the others, "Is forgiveness that's forced on us true forgiveness?" That question turns out to be the philosophical fulcrum that tilts the women toward their final decision. Their righteous anger means they can't forgive the men, and they are terrified their sons will grow up to emanate the men's behavior. So instead of offering forgiveness, they leave.

Many conversations about forgiveness hinge on the notion that forgiveness is freeing, either for the person granting it or its recipient. But what about the idea that not forgiving someone can also be freeing? What if we understood that forgiveness can be coerced? What if we stopped focusing on forgiveness as a *product*, and instead understood it as a *process*? *Women Talking* provokes us to consider what it means when forgiveness is essentially coerced or demanded. But that is often how forgiveness works. It is demanded of us. And that can lead to crippling bouts with self-doubt and guilt.

Most of the women in *Women Talking* don't know who assaulted them because they were knocked out with cow tranquilizers when the attacks happened. As it turns out, the men of the colony systematically perpetrated the rapes by cooperating with a local veterinarian who kept them supplied with the tranquilizer, and the men also clearly helped one another to access those drugs. For Polley, that question of whether we can even forgive something we can't or have tried hard not to remember should be part of our larger conversation about forgiveness and abuse. In *Run Toward the Danger*, she writes that our collective obsession with a victim's credibility is part of the problem. "I believe those women because the erratic way they behaved later, the inconsistencies in their stories, the gaps in their memories, all reminded me of my own behavior, my own memory."

The activist Tarana Burke coined the phrase "Me Too" in 2006, but it wasn't until 2017 that accusations about high-profile men like Bill O'Reilly, Harvey Weinstein, Larry Nassar, Kevin Spacey, Louis C. K., Al Franken, Matt Lauer, Woody Allen, and Mario Batali all arrived within a few months of one another. And while most of those men offered some kind of apology or mea culpa for what they had done, some, like Allen, have never admitted to doing anything wrong. Instead, a series of actors who'd worked with Allen came forward and apologized for ever associating with him, while he went on making films.

Six years later, as I sit here writing, men are still apologizing for abuse. #MeToo feels like a flashpoint, but also, sometimes, like a failure. Sarah Polley said a pivotal moment in her understanding of why the Mennonite women had to leave the colony to survive was knowing that the women "can't give forgiveness just because the men are asking for it." For all of the virality of #MeToo as an idea, and for the fact that it did manage to send a few truly vile men like Harvey Weinstein to prison, the world still expects victims to be forgiving just because men keep asking to be forgiven. To portray a group of women refusing this was the most radical thing a film could have done for many viewers of *Women Talking*.

It's also not the typical story we read about forgiveness. Americans are still obsessed with tidy endings, and the vaguer realities of forgiveness sometimes being a lifelong process, or forgiveness not being possible, aren't narratively satisfying. But they are realistic.

A 2010 poll by the Fetzer Institute revealed that more than half of Americans think there are situations that don't warrant forgiveness and that forgiveness should depend on the offender first apologizing and making changes. While depictions of a person deciding to forgive often focus on the individual, most poll respondents said they depended on friends, family, and community to help them come to a decision about forgiveness.

But the idea of universal, unconditional forgiveness persists. The Jesuit priest, writer, and activist Greg Boyle has worked with gang members in Los Angeles for decades through Homeboy Industries, the nonprofit he helped found. Homeboy members, often coming out of the mass incarceration system, receive counseling, legal assistance, classes, and job training. The program assists about ten thousand people a year, and Boyle's books and public speaking about his work have turned him into a celebrity in the Catholic world and beyond.

In 2022, Boyle published a book of devotionals illustrated by Fabian Devora, a muralist and painter from Los Angeles. The book is called *Forgive Everyone Everything*. I have to confess that the title made me uneasy when I first saw it. I was already working on this book, and I'm a big admirer of Boyle. I regularly recommend his book *Tattoos on the Heart*. But although we are both Catholics, we seem to disagree about forgiveness. *Forgive Everyone Everything* begins with a thesis. Boyle writes that "the way out to the place of resilience, the place of restoration, the place of not allowing your heart to be hardened by resentment, relies on one thing: forgive everyone everything."

Is this true? Maybe it is for Boyle, or for the people he works with, who range from murderers and drug dealers to rapists and petty thieves. And many of the people who wind up at Homeboy are themselves the victims of generational trauma, assault, mass incarceration, and systemic racism. So for them to be able to "forgive everyone everything" is truly miraculous. But while I still admire Boyle and the people he works with, I don't know if it is always true that it is possible or beneficial to forgive everything. I don't know if the victims of those Boyle works with forgive them, or if they struggle to do so, or if family members who've lost loved ones to gang violence can be that forgiving. "Forgive everyone everything" seems like an overly optimistic prescription that not many people can follow to the letter.

So if we can't always forgive everyone everything, what then? Are abused women like those in *Women Talking* really condemned to hell because they chose to leave instead of forgive? Would it even have been a real act of forgiveness for them to stay? And if someone is truly unapologetic or unrepentant, can they even really be forgiven? Are there real alternatives to forgiveness? What if we understood forgiveness not as a gesture or choice but as real, ongoing work? These are the questions we rarely ask. But we should.

***

Although American Christian understandings of forgiveness are at their core theoretically based on Jesus's teachings in the gospels, Jesus's own Jewishness has been so downplayed and even erased by American notions of assimilation, anti-Semitism, and white supremacy that many Christians have lost touch or have no understanding of how Jewish people like Jesus really understand forgiveness. This can be a lesson as we try to find alternatives to universal, reflexive forgiveness, which doesn't necessarily encourage us to change.

Rabbi Danya Ruttenberg has written widely on the Jewish understanding of atonement, and she draws from the medieval Jewish philosopher Mamonides in her book *On Repentance and Repair*. According to Ruttenberg, forgiveness is not the first step in the Jewish understanding of atonement and repentance. It's the *final* step. Repentance is work and process, and it requires multiple stages before forgiveness can be granted.

Maimonides's first step toward atonement is naming and owning the harm that was done "in as public a space as is warranted." The harm-doer must then demonstrate that they are actively working toward change, then offer restitution in some form, whether financial, psychological, or social, and accept the consequences of their actions. They then have to offer an apology, and not just once: Maimonides says that "they must appease and implore until [the harmed party] forgives them" and sometimes the harmed party just can't forgive, and that is alright. The final step, and the one perhaps least reflected in American Christian understandings of forgiveness, is that the harm-doer must commit to a lifetime of personal change, owning the harm they have done, but also, according to Ruttenberg, "owning the person that we are capable of becoming."

But a problem in our typical American conversations about forgiveness is, as Ruttenberg reminds us, that "real repentance requires real vulnerability, real risk." And, she adds, a pitfall of repentance work is doing it while still clinging to a position of power. You can easily point to any number of Hollywood celebrities who promised to take some time away and reflect after they'd been outed as abusive at the height of the #MeToo movement, but very few of them actually did this, and almost all of them complained about losing money, power, and privilege. The abuse crisis in the Catholic Church has bankrupted multiple dioceses and led to several church leaders who were found guilty of covering up or enabling abuse being pressured into stepping down. But very few of them have voluntarily given up their titles and the homes, cars, house cleaners, and private cooks that often come along with ecclesial employment in the upper ranks.

Americans don't like making sacrifices, as the pandemic has demonstrated, and the capitalist myth of a meritocracy where working hard is rewarded with riches and power means those who have both are reluctant to surrender them, feeling that they are "owed" a reward. But "we as a society," Rabbi Ruttenberg writes, "are not obligated to reward harmdoers with more opportunities to gain wealth, prestige, power, celebrity." This also translates to the idea of whether institutions and nations can be forgiven for historical harms. Reparations for slavery in America, for example, terrify some people in power because it would mean giving up money that was made as the result of generations of white privilege.

"Institutional courage" is the term Rabbi Ruttenberg uses for the willingness of an institution to surrender some of its power and privilege in order to make amends. Drilling names off buildings might be the first step in this process in some cases, but in more concrete examples, such as Georgetown University's promise to offer scholarships to the descendants of enslaved people owned by the Jesuits who founded the university, big talk led to minimal results. The plan was announced in 2016, and as of 2023, nothing has happened. Negest Rucker, a descendant of people enslaved by the Jesuit priests who founded Georgetown, said in 2021 that the Jesuits are "not sacrificing anything. So I don't see that as repair." And the Reverend Kelly Brown Douglas has said that many institutional gestures at repentance work are just that: gestures. "After the money has been paid," Rev. Douglas says, for the institution, "life goes on as usual."

The pressure put on people to forgive both institutions and individuals can actually be detrimental to the real work of repentance and the healing that work can bring. "In fact," according to Ruttenberg, "trying to put forgiveness ahead of healing has the potential to create more confusion and to prolong a process that requires time and tears, perhaps additional support, and certainly an honest grappling."

When the families of the people killed at Mother Emanuel in Charleston were praised for being so quick to forgive Dylann Roof, what was often glossed over in the coverage of their story were the less headline-grabbing interior processes each of those people went through and continue to go through, even after they may have publicly said they were forgiving. Grief and pain are not linear. Their faith may have taught them they needed to forgive to be with their loved ones in heaven, but that doesn't mean their suffering came to an abrupt end in that courtroom. Roof wrote a white supremacist manifesto in prison, which included the sentences "I do not regret what I did. I am not sorry." Because Roof never apologized and never repented, could he really have been forgiven in the first place? Nobody can know what is in the hearts and minds of the Mother Emanuel families but themselves. But we can understand that Dylan Roof did not express or seem to feel any remorse. So he did not want to be forgiven, and in turn, he was arguably not owed any forgiveness. Perhaps their gift of forgiveness was wasted on him. Perhaps not. Perhaps only God can know.

Restorative justice gives us another model that encourages us to consider forgiveness as a potential outcome of a process rather than an obligation owed to those who've done us harm. Howard Zehr, a criminologist who grew up in a Mennonite community, pioneered the restorative justice movement in America in the 1970s. But while restorative justice takes some cues from Mennonite notions of community reconciliation, Zehr has also acknowledged that the Maori people in New Zealand and First Nations people of Canada have traditions similar to restorative justice, which he draws upon.

At its core, the focus of restorative justice is not on punishment or forgiveness but on reconciliation. In his book *Changing Lenses*, Zehr describes six guiding questions for the process of restorative justice.

1. Who has been hurt?
2. What are their needs?
3. Whose obligations are these?
4. What are the causes?
5. Who has a stake in the situation?
6. What is the appropriate process to involve stakeholders in an effort to address causes and put things right?

Restorative justice was conceived as an answer to "weaknesses" of the Western legal system, primarily that its focus is on the breaking of laws and determining punishment. Zehr says that for proponents of restorative justice, "an area of special concern has been the neglect of victims and their needs; legal justice is largely about what to do with offenders."

Accountability, so little mentioned in conversations about forgiveness, is another focus of restorative justice. According to Zehr, "when a wrong has been done, it needs to be named and acknowledged. Those who have been harmed need to be able to grieve their losses, to be able to tell their stories, to have their questions answered." Instead of "obsessing" about whether offenders get the punishment they deserve or putting the focus on victims coming around to forgiving the person who harmed them, the restorative justice process is collaborative. It includes not just the offender and victim but community members participate as well. This model is similar to the South African concept of "ubuntu" that was a focus of that country's Truth and Reconciliation commission. Both ubuntu and restorative justice focus on interconnectedness, which puts the notion of mending the community alongside the needs of the individual, whether that person is the wrongdoer of the victim.

Lindsay Pointer, the associate director of the National Center on Restorative Justice, says that "rather than justice as 'punishment,' restorative justice conceives of justice as 'repair' to the harm caused by crime and conflict." According to Pointer, by including the needs of a community in the conversation, the restorative justice process helps to move beyond the punishment/forgiveness model and into a more collective conversation about what a community truly needs to feel like justice has been done.

The National Center on Restorative Justice also uses a model based on reflection and questions. In their restorative justice conversations, they first ask people to reflect on a time when they heard of a crime being committed in their community, and then to ask themselves what they needed as a community member. They then ask people to reflect on a time when they received significant harm and what their needs were at that time. Finally, they ask them to reflect on a time when you caused harm to another person and what your needs were at that time. As Pointer writes, this process reveals "there are some common human needs experienced in the wake of crime—needs for safety, understanding, validation, information, apology, and repair. These are needs that so often go completely unmet by our mainstream punitive justice responses, which are concerned primarily with assigning guilt and doling out punishments." What this process offers, Pointer says, is "a more holistic and humanizing view of what it means to pursue justice." It also means that for victims, in the restorative justice model, forgiveness is a potential outcome rather than a requirement, one potential endpoint of a process of healing rather than its beginning.

Restorative justice is put to work every day at Fremont High School, located in Oakland, California, where I grew up and continue to live. Like much of what locals call "Deep East" Oakland where Fremont High is located, the school's ethnic makeup is 98 percent students of color, and the neighborhood has the highest percentage of Oakland's average of about 3,000 shootings a year. Half of Fremont High's students are English language learners, and almost all are low income. In 2017, Fremont High had some of the school district's highest discipline rates and lowest attendance rates. Fights were common. 1 in 3 students dropped out. The same year, Oakland public schools made a 2.5-million-dollar investment in implementing restorative justice practices across the district, hoping it would transform schools like Fremont High. It did.

On Fremont High's restorative justice website, school leaders write that "in educational settings, RJ provides alternatives to punitive discipline, which in turn promotes positive school culture including safety, emphasis on learning and creativity, respect, and responsibility." The school uses three tiers of restorative justice: relate, repair, and restore. Conversation circles include students, teachers, and staff, and restore circles include students who have been suspended or who are returning from juvenile detention or extended absence. Fremont's model includes training students to lead restorative justice circles themselves, both at the school and at community events. School leaders write that in restorative justice circles, "we simultaneously address systemic forces of poverty, racial discrimination, intergenerational trauma, and other oppression," helping students to understand that justice and injustice occur on a continuum and that conversations about forgiveness should also acknowledge social and historical contexts.

Today, according to Tatiana Chaterji, the school's restorative justice coordinator, "we've worked so hard on building community, relationships, trust. I really feel we've made a difference." Fremont High's restorative justice program has been so successful that it has expanded to include district staff and community groups, and students now travel to national restorative justice conferences to give presentations. Significantly, the program no longer focuses only on conflict resolution but also applies the restorative justice model to bridge building between ethnic groups and student cliques. Fremont High students also now teach restorative justice circles to elementary school students at nearby Horace Mann School, where restorative justice coordinator Aaron Grey says that thanks to workshops with students from Fremont, "kids are resolving their own issues and organizing their own RJ circles. It's amazing to see. There's been a huge change in the culture."

Forgiveness also became a local topic of conversation when Jen Angel, who ran an Oakland bakery, was killed during a robbery in February of 2023. Angel, who had for years been involved in activism for prison abolition, worker's rights, BLM, and anti-war movements, died after being hurt by the fleeing vehicle of the person who robbed her. Immediately, Angel's friends and family issued a press release. It read, in part, that "Jen's values call for pursuing all available alternatives to traditional prosecution, such as restorative justice. Please do not use Jen's life legacy of care and community to further inflame narratives of fear, hatred and vengeance."

There was evidence to back this up, from Angel's refusal to call the police when someone threw a rock through the bakery window, to her years writing zines about progressive political issues, to her work to mobilize aid to homeless people in the West Oakland neighborhood where her bakery was located. When her friends' statement calling for restorative justice for her attacker went viral, there were outcries on social media that restorative justice or non-cooperation with police means "doing nothing." People on Twitter said anything from claiming that people asking for restorative justice "are endorsing the next criminal act of this kind" to arguing that "the cold-blooded [murderer] should be in prison for life." But Angel's partner Ocean Mottley, who is an attorney, clarified that Angel understood that the police system in America is racist and exacerbates existing social inequality. According to Mottley, Angel "would have wanted to find a way to heal our communities from this tragedy that didn't perpetuate more injustice." What this attitude reveals is that for people like Angel who believe in the restorative justice model, forgiveness being a process of amends-making, accountability, and communal repair may make them more forgiving in transformative ways than those who offer a shallow apology and empty forgiveness.

We can't know whether Jen Angel would have forgiven the person who robbed and killed her. But we do know that her example shows us that for some people, vengeance and punishment are not the solution. However, these concepts are so intrinsic to the idea of "justice" in a society where incarceration is seen as a solution to crime before rehabilitation of education that many failed to understand what exactly Angel's friends were asking for. They were not asking for the person who killed her to be forgiven, and they were not asking for that person to escape punishment altogether. Instead, they were asking for the restorative justice model of acknowledging the harm and understanding the needs of Angel's community alongside the needs of the person who did the harm.

When we reduce justice to simplistic notions of punishment or forgiveness, we can become blind to the institutional framework that leads to crime in the first place. What this means is that injustice continues to be perpetuated, and social issues like racism and poverty go unresolved. The same thing happens when people are pressured to forgive. The notion that this erases or vanquishes the harm done means we can turn a blind eye to anything from sexism and homophobia to the horrific way our nation handles mental illness, because once a victim of a crime "forgives" the perpetrator, the case is imagined to be closed. And that pattern just keeps repeating.

So, if not forgiveness, then what? Restorative justice is one model, and the notion of forgiveness as the potential outcome of a process of atonement is another one that decenters the person who has done the harm and recenters the victim and the community. There is also the possibility that we just need a broader conversation about what we mean when we talk about forgiveness. I want to return to the work of Jeanne Safer, the psychologist whose book

Forgiving and Not Forgiving also offers alternatives to a simplistic, automatic kind of forgiveness. Toward the end of her book, Safer says, "We need a more forgiving definition of forgiveness," one that is more flexible and more compassionate. Safer expands on this further:

> The doctrine of universal forgiveness is one-size-fits-all absolutism. Encouraging people to strive for this unrealistic goal— even when the motive is salvaging their psyches or saving their souls—instills negative feelings of inadequacy in anyone who fails to achieve it. Worse, it encourages false forgiveness, which threatens to inundate our public as well as our private lives. The question "Does this person deserve to be forgiven and am I able to do it?" should not be taboo. To insist on forgiveness in all cases is to confuse forgiving with resolving, to equate unforgiveness with vengefulness, and to ignore the critical role subjectivity plays in determining what is forgivable and what is not.

***

The unfortunate outcome of our rigid understanding of forgiveness, both in religion and in secular culture, is guilt. As a cradle Catholic born into an Irish Catholic family, I have a legacy case of Catholic guilt that goes generations deep. Catholic guilt is a special mixture of shame and self-loathing formed in a catechesis laser-focused on sins of the body and on insisting that every harm done to you must be forgiven. And I can also recognize that one reason Christianity in America is hemorrhaging members, with churches and Christian schools shuttering everywhere we look, is that people are sick of feeling guilty. Some degree of guilt is useful, of course, for keeping our moral compass in check and for helping us to recognize when we perpetuate injustice or do someone else harm.

But feeling guilty about not being able to forgive everyone everything is exhausting. It is a heavy burden to bear hearing that you're damning yourself or sentencing yourself to a lifetime of suffering because something so heinous was done to you that you cannot release the harm-doer from their own guilt. The connection of not being able to forgive to a person being obsessed with vengeance or wrath is also an oversimplification. Not every case of forgiveness having limits leads to a revenge fantasy being lived out or a guilty penitent lying on their deathbed, expressing regret that they could not forgive someone. The reality is often much more mundane, just untold people going on with their lives without absolving others who hurt them. And if your understanding is that God is all-forgiving, insisting that everyone should also be all-forgiving is, in a way, insisting that each of us should be exactly like God. We would all fall short by this measure.

The guilt felt by the victim who struggles to forgive is misplaced. A rapist or sexual abuser should feel guilty. A murderer should feel guilty. A person who participates in racism or homophobia should feel guilty. The person who is damaged, whether by individuals or by systems, should not. When we forgive people who do us harm, we need to ask ourselves and them what this insistence on forgiveness is really doing to bring healing to them, to ourselves, and to our communities. Is our insistence on being forgiven selfish, an attempt to alleviate our own guilt? Do we have to call it forgiveness every single time, insist it operate on a timeline, or believe that people who are quick to forgive are in some way morally better?

The fact is that Safer is right, and we need a better definition of forgiveness, one less tied up in guilt and punishment and more focused on our mutual work to better our communities and world. And we need to understand that sometimes it is simply okay to say, "I can't forgive this person, or this institution, or this historical wrong. I can't even promise that I'll get there eventually. I'll try, but there's no guarantee. And, by the way, this does not make me a bad person or a failure." When someone hurts us and says, "Please forgive me," we need to get comfortable taking time to reply. Maybe even years. Maybe lifetimes. Maybe never. There are harms done that cannot be forgiven, and we need to acknowledge that, even while we also acknowledge that our understanding of forgiveness needs to evolve. Because if the ultimate goal of forgiveness is freeing ourselves from a burden, not being able to forgive should lead to a kind of freedom too. If forgiveness is supposed to be about reconciliation, community, and a return to wholeness for the person who has been wronged, for some people, withholding of forgiveness can be a pathway toward the same freedom and reconciliation that forgiveness promises.

At the end of *Women Talking*, the Mennonite women take the children, the furniture, the chickens, and the rest of the food they'll need. And they leave behind the men who hurt them, who systematically planned together to drug and rape them, because those men cannot be forgiven. For these women, forgiveness would not only mean that they and their daughters would go on being punished but that the next generation of men would also grow up believing their own abuse would be forgiven too. So, they don't forgive. But the women load their wagons and hitch their horses and set off on a single-track path between fields, toward a new kind of life.

Acknowledgments

Writing one book during a pandemic is difficult. Writing two has felt, on more than one occasion, like an impossible task. Yet here is the second book of COVID-19 (may we someday soon see the end of it), and it would not have arrived without the help of the following people.

Thanks to everyone at Broadleaf, for making both this book and *The Defiant Middle* a reality, and for being such an amenable and thoughtful publisher to work with. I'm especially grateful to Andrew DeYoung, for stepping in as editor and helping shape the final version of this book.

In 2007, I was a sad poet occasionally writing essays who got an email from a literary agent asking if I'd ever thought about writing a nonfiction book. I had not, and yet, here's the fifth one. Thank you, Michelle Brower, for seeing potential in my work, and for the hard work you do on behalf of so many writers.

Since 1999, I've worked at UC Berkeley and have had the privilege of teaching thousands of students. It's impossible to name every one of you, but I'm grateful that the work of teaching people about reading and writing is such a life-giving job, thanks to you. Thank you to all of my colleagues in the College Writing Programs, and to our support staff, with special thanks to my fellow creative writing faculty, my officemates, and friends in the program. I want to give a shoutout to my late colleague Steve Tollefson, who taught me everything I know about teaching. I also want to thank Dr. Rohnit Stahl and the Othering and Belonging Institute at Berkeley, for supporting my last book, and the Berkeley libraries and librarians, for being such generous caretakers of knowledge.

Some of the early material here was workshopped at a Collegeville Institute gathering that was moved online due to COVID-19. Thanks to the writers and editors in that group who responded to the earliest ideas in this book (at 7 a.m. on Zoom), particularly to Jessica Mesman. I also started thinking through some of these ideas when preparing to speak at a panel on clergy abuse at the Academy of American Religion conference in 2019. Thanks to the other panelists and organizers, for inviting me, and to all of the schools and churches where I've given talks in the past few years (and to Rev. Molly Baskette, Rev. Kara Slade, Dr. Annie Selak, Dr. Sundari Johansen-Hurwitt, Chris Stedman, Fr. Shannon TL Kearns and Brian Murphy, and many more people who have invited and collaborated with me on events and podcasts).

Religion writers have turned out to be the most exceedingly generous and supportive colleagues a person could ask for. Thank you to Matthew Sitman, who was around for the very beginning of this book, and everyone at *Killing the Buddha*, especially former editor Brook Willensky-Lanford, for publishing a very early excerpt from this book. Kerry Weber, Jim Keane, Mike O'Louglin, Tim Reidy, Jim Martin, Paddy Gilger, and many more people at/from/ around *America Magazine* have supported my work for over a decade. Thanks to Evan Dercakz and Lisa Webster of *Religion Dispatches*, who helped me find a beat and a voice in religion writing, and to Brendan Walsh at *The Tablet*, for supporting *The Defiant Middle*. Thanks also to the editors of *Commonweal*. Special thanks to Brett Krutzch at *The Revealer*, who suggested I start writing a column when I complained on Twitter that I didn't have one (dreams come true, but only if you complain first), and who has been a huge support as I worked on several columns that formed the backbone of this book. Katelyn Beaty was also present at the gestation of this book, and Lil Copan helped shape the proposal. Thanks to them as well.

Every author I've cited in this book deserves thanks, and I hope readers will check out their work. While I didn't end up directly quoting from or paraphrasing them, I also listened to a lot of podcasts that helped me think through some of the topics I wrote about here. Thanks to the hosts and researchers of *Stuff You Should Know*, *Let's Talk About Sects*, *Throughline*, *You're Wrong About*, *Stuff the British Stole*, *Fall of Civilizations*, *Violation*, *The Retrievals*, *Maintenance Phase*, and *Presidential*, for talking about forgiveness in nuanced and interesting ways.

Just as this book went into production, I was diagnosed with a life-changing illness. My medical team has been astonishingly quick about getting me into treatment, and it's thanks to them that I'm still here. Thank you also to friends who continue to show up for me: Sam, Stefanie, Bean, Mark, Debbie, Julia, Nate, Jason, Greg, Carlo, Mary, Mike, John, Kim, Laurel, Michael, Jeremy, Dylan, Jen, and so many more people in my personal communion of saints. Thank you also to everyone who has supported my work online and in person, whether through writing reviews, sharing things on social media, sending emails, using my books in book clubs, or buying copies as gifts. I never imagined having an audience, and as it turns out, I have the best one.

I'm so grateful to work with Dale Trunk, who helped me think through many ideas in this book. Lucie Tetrault also helped sustain my mental health for many, many years, and I owe her much gratitude.

My family remains the root of everything I write. Thank you, mom, Betsy (with special thanks to you and Kerry for giving me a place to write), Robert, Christine, Vicki, Jennifer, Melanie, Ava, Lior, and Avi. Thanks to my late father, Leo, for always encouraging me to read more, and my late grandparents, for being a model of sustained mutual support. Thanks to Sage, for putting up with me for twenty-five years. Not everyone survives being married to a writer, but you make it look easy(ish).

Notes

Introduction

xii   *The late theologian James Cone wrote:* Jennifer Berry Hawes, *Grace Will Lead Us Home: The Charleston Church Massacre and the Hard, Inspiring Journey to Forgiveness* (New York: St. Martin's Press, 2019).

xiii   *And Felicia Sanders, whose son was dead:* Hawes, *Grace Will Lead Us Home,* 74–75.

xiii   *At the crescendo of his eulogy:* Office of the Press Secretary, "Remarks by the President in Eulogy for the Honorable Reverend Clementa Pinckney," Obama White House, June 26, 2015, https://obamawhitehouse.archives.gov/the-press-office/2015/06/26/remarks-president-eulogy-honorable-reverend-clementa-pinckney.

xiv   *The story of forgiveness in Charleston:* Hawes, *Grace Will Lead Us Home,* 92.

xiv   *Roof, who claimed to have read:* Frances Robles, "Dylann Roof Photos and a Manifesto Are Posted on Website," *New York Times,* June 20, 2015, https://www.nytimes.com/2015/06/21/us/dylann-storm-roof-photos-website-charleston-church-shooting.html.

Chapter 1

5   *While many portrayals of forgiveness:* Ibid.

6   *In Griswold's argument:* Charles Griswold, *Forgiveness: A Philosophical Exploration* (New York: Cambridge University Press, 2007).

6   *But even if reconciliation isn't always possible, Stanford Encyclopedia of Philosophy:* (Stanford, CA: Stanford University, 1997).

6   *Bishop Desmond Tutu:* Luke 8:17, NRSV.

7   *Philosopher Richard Swinburne writes:* Richard Swinburne, "Forgiving as a Performative Utterance," in *Forgiveness and Its Moral Dimensions*, ed. Brandon Warmke, Dana Kay Nelkin, and Michael McKenna (Oxford University Press, 2021).

9   *According to Luskin:* Fred Luskin, "What Is Forgiveness?" *Greater Good Magazine*, August 19, 2010, https://greatergood.berkeley.edu/article/item/what_is_forgiveness.

11 *The US Department of Veterans:* Sonya B. Norman, PhD, and Shira Maguen, PhD, "Moral Injury," PTSD: National Center for PTSD, https://www.ptsd.va.gov/professional/treat/cooccurring/moral_injury.asp#:~:text=Moral%20injury%20is%20the%20distressing,individual's%20values%20and%20moral%20beliefs.

12 *One study by psychiatrists:* Suzette Brémault-Phillips, Terry Cherwick, Lorraine Alison Smith-MacDonald, John Huh, and Eric Vermetten, "Forgiveness: A Key Component of Healing from Moral Injury?" *Frontiers in Psychiatry* 13 (2022): https://www.frontiersin.org/articles/10.3389/fpsyt.2022.906945/full#B43.

13 *My friend Katya's:* Name changed at her request.

14 *This is also true for my friend Mary:* Not her real name. Changed at her request.

16 *Rachel says Peter became:* Nancy Updike, *We Were Three*, October 11, 2022, produced by Jenelle Pifer and Nancy Updike, podcast, https://www.nytimes.com/2022/10/11/podcasts/we-were-three.html.

19 *The death penalty is legal:* Wendy Sawyer and Peter Wagner, "Mass Incarceration: The Whole Pie 2022," Prison Policy Initiative, March 14, 2022, https://www.prisonpolicy.org/reports/pie2022.html.

Chapter 2

22 *People in Plymouth Colony:* Caleb Johnson, "Crime and Punishment in Plymouth Colony," MayflowerHistory.com, accessed October 23, 2023, http://mayflowerhistory.com/crime.

22 *Sewall said he would:* Bill of Rights Institute, "Asking Pardon of Men: Samuel Sewall and Responsibility—Handout A: Narrative,"

https://billofrightsinstitute.org/activities/asking-pardon-of-men-samuel-sewall-and-responsibility-handout-a-narrative.

24 *For Augustine, who believed sin was a human creation:* Saint Augustine, *The Confessions of Saint Augustine,* trans. E. B. Pusey (Project Gutenberg, 2001), https://www.gutenberg.org/files/3296/3296-h/3296-h.htm.

25 *Consequently it is a mortal sin generically:* St. Thomas Aquinas, *Summa Theologica,* trans. Fathers of the English Dominican Province (Benziger Bros., 1947), https://ccel.org/ccel/aquinas/summa/summa.i.html.

26 *On the day of his execution:* Chas Sisk, "Donnie Johnson Executed for 1984 Murder of His Wife," *WPLN News,* May 17, 2019, https://wpln.org/post/donnie-johnson-executed-for-1984-murder-of-his-wife/.

27 *His stepdaughter was more:* Katherine Burgess, "Their Father Killed Their Mother. Now, the Siblings Disagree on Whether He Should Be Executed." *The Tennessean,* May 8, 2019, https://www.tennessean.com/story/news/2019/05/08/donnie-johnson-death-row-inmate-children-disagree-whether-he-should-be-executed/3654731002/.

29 *At the height of the Boston scandal:* Deborah Beker, "Irish Catholics Call for Cardinal Law's Resignation, Following Clergy Abuse Report," *WBUR,* February 10, 2010, https://www.wbur.org/news/2010/02/10/irish-priests-followup.

29 *The presiding cardinal:* Angelo Beker, "Irish Catholics Call."

30 *In an essay entitled:* Karen Lebacqz, "Love Your Enemy: Sex, Power, and Christian Ethics," *The Annual Society of Christian Ethics* 10 (1990): 3–23, https://www.jstor.org/stable/23560724.

31 *In the Christian tradition:* Serene Jones, "A Terrorist War against Women," *Sojourners,* February 2018, https://sojo.net/magazine/february-2018/terrorist-war-against-women.

31 *In terms of sexual violence:* Jones, "A Terrorist War."

31 *For Jones, the challenge:* Jones, "A Terrorist War."

31 *In an essay entitled "Preaching Forgiveness?":* John S. McClure and Nancy J. Ramsay, eds., *Telling the Truth: Preaching about Sexual Abuse and Forgiveness* (Cleveland, OH: United Church Press, 1998).

31 *According to her, forgiveness:* McClure and Nancy, *Telling the Truth.*

32 *Forgiveness is not:* McClure and Nancy, *Telling the Truth.*

32 *In her book Enfleshing Freedom:* M. Shawn Copeland, *Enfleshing Freedom: Body, Race and Being* (Minneapolis: Fortress Press, 2009).

32 *These women could not:* Copeland, *Enfleshing Freedom.*

32 *Rather, when Prejean:* Copeland, *Enfleshing Freedom.*

33 *While the Old English forgiefan means:* Online Etymology Dictionary, "Forgive (v.)," updated August 9, 2023, https://www.etymonline.com/word/forgive.

33 *Merriam Webster's modern definition:* Merriam-Webster.com Dictionary, "Forgive," updated October 13, 2023, https://www.merriam-webster.com/dictionary/forgive.

34 *Rather than meaning something like:* Bible Study Tools, "Aphiemi," accessed October 23, 2023, https://www.biblestudytools.com/lexicons/greek/nas/aphiemi.html.

34 *In Matthew's version of the Lord's Prayer:* Blue Letter Bible, "Matthew 6 (KJV)," https://www.blueletterbible.org/kjv/mat/6/12/t_conc_935012.

34 *YHWH will "remove sin:* J. J. Stamm, "slḥ," in vol. 2 of *Theological Lexicon of the Old Testament*, ed. Ernst Jenni and Claus Westermann, trans. Mark E. Biddle (Peabody, MA: Hendrickson, 2004), 797–803. Thanks to Dr. Tom Bolin for this reference.

34 *Who pardons [ha-soleakh] all your iniquities:* Sarah E. Fisher, "Salakh: Forgive and Forget," *Hebrew Word Lessons* (blog), September 27, 2020, https://hebrewwordlessons.com/2020/09/27/salakh-forgive-and-forget/#:~:text=FORGIVE%2FPARDON%2D%20salakh.,verb.

36 *Slicha does not include a requirement:* Danya Ruttenberg, *On Repentance and Repair* (Boston: Beacon Press, 2022), 171–72.

36 *Dr. Thomas Bolin, a scholar of the Hebrew Bible:* Thanks to Dr. Bolin, for talking to me both on the phone and via email.

36 *Biblical scholar David Lambert also describes:* David A. Lambert, *How Repentance Became Biblical: Judaism, Christianity, and the Interpretation of Scripture* (New York: Oxford University Press, 2015).

37 *The early church fathers:* Bart D. Ehrman, *Jesus Before the Gospels: How the Earliest Christians Remembered, Changed, and Invented Their Stories of the Savior* (New York: HarperOne, 2016).

39 *But in order to achieve the Teshuvah:* Rabbi Moshe ben Maimon, "Teshuva—Chapter Two," in *Mishneh Torah (Rambam)*, trans. Eliyahu Touger, https://www.chabad.org/library/article_cdo/aid/911891/jewish/Teshuvah-Chapter-Two.htm.

41 *Ubuntu, Tutu writes:* Desmond Tutu, *No Future without Forgiveness* (New York: Random House, 1999), 35.

Chapter 3

46 *The Black writer Ishmael Reed:* Hua Hsu, "In 'The Haunting of Lin-Manuel Mirandaa,' Ishmael Reed Revives an Old Debate," *New Yorker*, January 9, 2019, https://www.newyorker.com/culture/cultural-comment/in-the-haunting-of-lin-manuel-miranda-ishmael-reed-revives-an-old-debate.

46 *Hamilton, who Chernow says had:* Kyle Swenson, "America's First 'Hush Money' Scandal: Alexander Hamilton's Torrid Affair with

Maria Reynolds," *Washington Post*, March 23, 2018, https://www.washingtonpost.com/news/morning-mix/wp/2018/03/23/americas-first-hush-money-scandal-alexander-hamiltons-torrid-affair-with-maria-reynolds/.

46 *In the musical and in history:* Founders Online, "Printed Version of the 'Reynolds Pamphlet', 1797," National Archives, accessed October 23, 2023, https://founders.archives.gov/documents/Hamilton/01-21-02-0138-0002.

49 *As an adult, he almost never attended church:* Founders Online, "Alexander Hamilton's Final Version of the Report on the Subject of Manufactures, [5 December 1791]," National Archives, accessed October 23, 2023, https://founders.archives.gov/documents/Hamilton/01-10-02-0001-0007.

50 *The young German monk Martin Luther:* David B. Morris, "Martin Luther as Priest, Heretic, and Outlaw: The Reformation at 500," European Reading Room, Library of Congress, accessed October 23, 2023, https://www.loc.gov/rr/european/luther.html.

50 *In the eighty-sixth thesis, Luther writes:* "The 95 Theses," www.LUTHER.de, 1997, https://www.luther.de/en/95thesen.html.

51 *Perhaps the greatest influence on this thinking:* "Book 3–Chapter 4 (Parts1–2)," John Calvin for Everyone, accessed October 23, 2023, http://www.johncalvinforeveryone.org/chapter-4-parts-1-21.html

52 *To be forgiven:* "Book 3."

52 *Calvin also thought that:* "Table of Contents," Calvin's Institutes, Christian Classics Ethereal Library, accessed October 23, 2023, https://www.ccel.org/ccel/calvin/institutes.toc.html.

52 *According to Voltaire, Reformers:* www.cristoraul.com/ENGLISH/Universal-Literature/Voltaire-Works/Works-of-Voltaire-Volume-27.html.

53 *He rejected Luther's notion:* Susan Doran, "Henry VIII and the Reformation," *Discovering Sacred Texts*, British Library, September 23, 2019, https://www.bl.uk/sacred-texts/articles/henry-viii-and-the-reformation.

53 *Instead of the Catholic notion:* https://twitter.com/cebm__.

55 *The danger was that:* James Hennesey, *American Catholics: A History of the Roman Catholic Community in the United States* (Oxford: Oxford University Press, 1981), https://archive.org/details/americancatholic00henn/page/119/mode/2up.

55 *By the time John F. Kennedy:* "John F. Kennedy Address to the Greater Houston Ministerial Association," AmericanRhetoric.com, accessed September 11, 2007, https://web.archive.org/web/20070911175450/http://www.americanrhetoric.com/speeches/jfkhoustonministers.html.

56 ***Kennedy wasn't exactly a perfect Catholic:*** www.cnn.com/2013/11/22/politics/gallery/jfk-catholic/index.html.

57 ***The Book of Mormon seems to portray:*** The Church of Jesus Christ of Latter-Day Saints, "Forgiveness," Topics and Questions, accessed October 23, 2023, https://www.churchofjesuschrist.org/study/manual/gospel-topics/forgiveness?lang=eng.

57 ***Joseph Smith also wrote that:*** The Church of Jesus Christ of Latter-Day Saints, "Joseph Smith—History," Pearl of Great Price, Scriptures, accessed October 23, 2023, https://www.churchofjesuschrist.org/study/scriptures/pgp/js-h/1.29?lang=eng#p29.

57 ***Latter Day Saints don't practice confession:*** Bishop J. Richard Clarke, "Confession," Magazines, The Church of Jesus Christ of Latter-Day Saints, November 1980, https://www.churchofjesuschrist.org/study/new-era/1980/11/confession?lang=eng.

58 ***Norman Vincent Peale, pastor to:*** Norman Vincent Peale, "When Faced with the Need to Forgive," *Guideposts* (blog), accessed October 23, 2023, https://www.guideposts.org/better-living/positive-living/when-faced-with-the-need-to-forgive.

58 ***Billy Graham, perhaps America's:*** Billy Graham Library, "10 Quotes from Billy Graham on Forgiveness," February 7, 2020, https://billygrahamlibrary.org/blog-10-quotes-from-billy-graham-on-forgiveness/.

59 ***Writing to the Jesuit priest:*** https://www.catholicworker.org/526-html.

59 ***That same summer, Scott Hancock:*** Scott Hancock, "The Limits of Black Forgiveness," *Journal of the Civil War Era*, June 19, 2020, https://www.journalofthecivilwarera.org/2020/06/the-limits-of-black-forgiveness/.

60 ***Beneath this narrative, however:*** Hancock, "The Limits of Black Forgiveness,"

61 ***In one article on the History Channel website:*** Erin Blakemore, "Frederick Douglass's Emotional Meeting with the Man Who Enslaved Him," *HISTORY*, January 28, 2021, https://www.history.com/news/frederick-douglass-meeting-former-master.

61 ***And a Christian blogger refers:*** Bobby Valentine, "Stories of Grace, Stories of Forgiveness: Frederick Douglass Affirms the Humanity of a Slaveholder," *Stoned-Campbell Disciple* (blog), March 4, 2013, https://stonedcampbelldisciple.com/2013/03/04/stories-of-grace-stories-of-forgiveness-frederick-douglass-affirms-the-humanity-of-a-slaveholder/.

61 ***"Well the nation may forget":*** David Blight, *Frederick Douglass' Civil War* (Louisiana State University Press, 1989), 224.

61 ***According to the historian Robert Levine:*** Robert S. Levine, "Frederick Douglass and Thomas Auld: Reconsidering the Reunion Narrative," *The Journal of African American History* 99 (2014): 1–2, 34–45.

62 ***Levine writes that while:*** Levine, "Frederick Douglass."

62 *With this idea of an audience:* Daryl Austin, "'This Is Not a Lesson in Forgiveness.' Why Frederick Douglass Met with His Former Enslaver," *National Geographic*, December 2, 2020, https://www.nationalgeographic.com/history/article/not-lesson-forgiveness-why-frederick-douglass-met-former-enslaver.

62 *Noelle Trent of the National Civil Rights:* Austin, "'This Is Not a Lesson.'"

63 *Trent adds that the meeting of:* Austin, "'This Is Not a Lesson.'"

63 *Ka'mal McClarin, a historian:* Austin, "'This Is Not a Lesson.'"

63 *When Ona Judge escaped:* "Ona Judge," Digital Encyclopedia, George Washington's Mount Vernon, accessed October 23, 2023, https://www.mountvernon.org/library/digitalhistory/digital-encyclopedia/article/ona-judge/.

Chapter 4

66 *For people who have survived abuse:* Kurt Smith, "Why You Should Forgive but 'Never' Forget," *PsychCentral*, updated April 5, 2022, https://psychcentral.com/health/reasons-to-forgive-but-not-forget#what-does-it-mean.

66 *A 2015 study by psychologists:* Stephanie Lichtenfeld, Vanessa L. Buechner, Markus A. Maier, and Maria Fernández-Capo, "Forgive and Forget: Differences between Decisional and Emotional Forgiveness," *PLoS One* 10, no. 5 (2015): https://www.ncbi.nlm.nih.gov/pmc/articles/PMC4422736/.

66 *But while most psychologists argue:* James K. McNulty, "The Dark Side of Forgiveness: The Tendency to Forgive Predicts Continued Psychological and Physical Aggression in Marriage," *Pers Soc Psychol Bull* 37, no. 6 (June 2011): https://www.ncbi.nlm.nih.gov/pmc/articles/PMC4112745/.

69 *Some Native people once brought:* Maynard Geiger, *The Life and Times of Fray Junípero Serra: The Man Who Never Turned Back*, vol. 1 (WA: Academy of American Franciscan History, 1959) 233, 235–36.

70 *On August 29, 1911:* Facts about Ishi's life taken from Phoebe A. Hearst Museum of Anthropology, "Ishi," accessed October 23, 2023, https://hearstmuseum.berkeley.edu/ishi/.

71 *Stripped of any context:* James Clifford, *Returns: Becoming Indigenous in the 21st Century* (Cambridge, MA: Harvard University Press, 2013), 95.

73 *The pope described Serra as:* Pope Francis, "Holy Mass and Canonization of Blessed Fr. Junípero Serra: Holimy of His Holiness Pope Francis," Holy See Press Office, September 23, 2015, https://www.vatican.va/content/francesco/en/homilies/2015/documents/papa-francesco_20150923_usa-omelia-washington-dc.html.

73 *But for Native activist:* Carly Severn, "'How Do We Heal?' Toppling the Myth of Junípero Serra," *KQED*, July 7, 2020, https://www.kqed.org/news/11826151/how-do-we-heal-toppling-the-myth-of-junipero-serra.

74 *Instead, he called the activists:* CBS San Francisco, "San Francisco Archbishop Holds Exorcism at Golden Gate Park Site Where Serra Statue Was Toppled," *CBS News*, June 30, 2020, https://www.cbsnews.com/sanfrancisco/news/san-francisco-archbishop-exorcism-golden-gate-park-junipero-serra-statue-toppled/.

74 *Cordileone performed an exorcism:* CBS San Francisco, "San Francisco Archbishop."

75 *Nicholas Flood Davin, a Canadian politician:* Erin Hanson, "The Residential School System," indigenousfoundations.arts.ubc.ca, published 2009, updated September 2020, https://indigenousfoundations.arts.ubc.ca/the_residential_school_system/#:~:text=The%20residential%20school%20system%20officially,to%20speak%20their%20own%20languages.

75 *And anywhere between half:* Hanson, "The Residential School System."

75 *"The Government of Canada,":* "Prime Minister Harper Offers Full Apology on Behalf of Canadians for the Indian Residential Schools System," *Government of Canada*, June 11, 2008, https://www.rcaanc-cirnac.gc.ca/eng/1100100015644/1571589171655.

75 *"It wasn't good enough":* Kerry Benjoe, "Group Gathers for Harper's Apology," *Leader-Post*, June 12, 2008, https://web.archive.org/web/20120915023426/http://www2.canada.com/reginaleaderpost/news/story.html?id=2e362bf9-0f5a-43c6-ab5e-81a276b4767c.

76 *Calling the residential schools:* Nicole Winfield and Peter Smith, "Pope Apologizes for 'Catastrophic' School Policy in Canada," *AP News*, July 26, 2022, https://apnews.com/article/pope-francis-canada-apology-visit-137ad23719603e9d370257f257ec0163.

77 *According to Sinclair, the pope's apology:* Rachel Bergen, "Pope's Apology Doesn't Acknowledge Church's Role as 'Co-Author' of Dark Chapter: Murray Sinclair," *CBC News*, July 26, 2022, https://www.cbc.ca/news/canada/manitoba/murray-sinclair-pope-apology-1.6532525.

78 *Physical aftereffects of trauma:* Bessel van der Kolk, *The Body Keeps the Score: Brain, Mind and Body in the Healing of Trauma* (New York: Penguin, 2015).

78 *Because they've experienced trauma:* van der Kolk, *The Body Keeps the Score.*

78 *In an article in Indian Country magazine:* Dina Gilio-Whitaker, "Is Forgiveness the Only Option to Heal from Historical Trauma?" *Indian Country Today*, August 25, 2016, https://indiancountrytoday.com/archive/is-forgiveness-the-only-option-to-heal-from-historical-trauma.

78 *The play posed the question:* Gilio-Whitaker, "Is Forgiveness the Only Option."

79 *On a collective level:* Gilio-Whitaker, "Is Forgiveness the Only Option."

79 *Instead of asking people stuck:* Gilio-Whitaker, "Is Forgiveness the Only Option."

81 *The person being asked for forgiveness:* Gilio-Whitaker, "Is Forgiveness the Only Option."

Chapter 5

83 *Archbishop Blair held a special:* Rick Rojas, "Catholic Archbishop, on His Hands and Knees, Begged for Forgiveness Over Abuse," *New York Times*, March 8, 2019, https://www.nytimes.com/2019/03/08/nyregion/reparation-masses.html.

84 *"Apologies," Ingala said:* Rojas, "Catholic Archbishop."

84 *Among the reader comments:* Rojas, "Catholic Archbishop."

87 *By the end of the following year:* Sarah Larson, "'Spotlight' and Its Revelations," *New Yorker*, December 8, 2015, https://www.newyorker.com/culture/sarah-larson/spotlight-and-its-revelations.

87 *Walter Robinson, one of the original Spotlight:* Larson, "'Spotlight' and Its Revelations."

87 *Psychologists who work with victims:* Rosaleen McElvaney, Rusan Lateef, Delphine Collin-Vézina, Ramona Alaggia, and Megan Simpson, "Bringing Shame out of the Shadows: Identifying Shame in Child Sexual Abuse Disclosure Processes and Implications for Psychotherapy," Journal of Interpersonal Violence 37 (2021): https://journals.sagepub.com/doi/10.1177/08862605211037435.

87 *In their article:* Prachi H. Bhuptani and Terri L. Messman-Moore, "Blame and Shame in Sexual Assault," *Handbook of Sexual Assault and Sexual Assault Prevention* (2019): 309–322, https://link.springer.com/chapter/10.1007/978-3-030-23645-8_18.

88 *For centuries, clericalism has led to:* Martin Luther, Henry Eyster, and Adolph Spaeth, Works of Martin Luther, with Introductions and Notes (Philadelphia: A.J. Holman, 1915), https://archive.org/details/worksmartinluth00spaegoog/page/n307/mode/2up.

88 *Pope Francis has called clericalism:* Zenit Staff, "Pope Francis' Address to the Synod Fathers at Opening of Synod2018 on Young People, the Faith and Vocational Dscernment," *Zenit*, October 3, 2018, https://zenit.org/2018/10/03/pope-francis-address-to-the-synod-fathers-at-opening-of-synod2018-on-young-people-the-faith-and-vocational-discernment/.

90 *He apologized, and he told clergy:* "Cardinal Law Apologizes, begs Forgiveness," *CNN*, December 16, 2002, https://www.cnn.com/2002/US/Northeast/12/16/cardinal.law/index.html.

90 *What he did not tell us:* Angela Kennecka, "Sioux Falls Priest Accused of Sexual Harassment Resigns Vatican Position," *KELOLAND News*,

December 7, 2017, https://www.keloland.com/news/investigates/sioux-falls-priest-accused-of-sexual-harassment-resigns-vatican-position/.

91 ***When that story broke in 2017:*** Angela Kennecka, "Allegations of Sexual Harassment against Sioux Falls Priest," *KELOLAND News*, June 27, 2017, https://www.keloland.com/news/investigates/allegations-of-sexual-harassment-agai nst-sioux-falls-priest/.

91 ***Pope Benedict was most likely:*** Alexander Stille, "What Pope Benedict Knew about Abuse in the Catholic Church," *New Yorker*, January 14, 2016, https://www.newyorker.com/news/news-desk/what-pope-benedict-knew-about-abuse-in-the-catholic-church.

92 ***One German advocate for:*** Sylvia Poggioli, "Pope Benedict XVI Apologizes for Handling of Sexual Abuse Cases but Denies Wrongdoing," *NPR*, February 9, 2022, https://www.npr.org/2022/02/09/1079655013/pope-benedict-xvi-apologizes-for-handling-of-sexual-abuse-cases-but-denies-wrong.

92 ***According to Annie Selak:*** Annie Selak, "Pope Francis Apologized for the Harm Done to First Nations Peoples, but What Does a Pope's Apology Mean?" *Religion News Service*, April 8, 2022, https://religionnews.com/2022/04/08/pope-francis-apologized-for-the-harm-done-to-first-nations-peoples-but-what-does-a-popes-apology-mean/.

93 ***But he was expelled from:*** Jason Berry, "Father Marcial Maciel and the Popes He Stained," *Newsweek*, March 11, 2013, https://www.newsweek.com/father-marcial-maciel-and-popes-he-stained-62811.

94 ***An investigation later found:*** BBC News, "Marcial Maciel: Mexican Founder Legionaries of Christ 'Abused 60 Minors,'" *BBC News*, December 22, 2019, https://www.bbc.com/news/world-latin-america-50884518.

94 ***Maciel fathered at least six children:*** Jason Berry, "How Fr. Maciel Built His Empire," *National Catholic Reporter*, April 12, 2010, https://www.ncronline.org/news/accountability/how-fr-maciel-built-his-empire.

95 ***This same propensity to look:*** Thanks to Tony Ginnochio, whose newsletter Grifts of the Holy Spirit helped me put some of these stories about McCarrick together.

96 ***But for decades, McCarrick:*** Elizabeth Dias, Ruth Graham, and Liam Stack, "Ex-Cardinal McCarrick Faces Milestone Charges in Catholic Sex Abuse Crisis," July 29, 2021, https://www.nytimes.com/2021/07/29/us/cardinal-mccarrick-sexual-abuse-charge.html.

97 ***According to Graham:*** Ruth Graham, "Theodore McCarrick Still Won't Confess," *Slate*, September 3, 2019, https://slate.com/human-interest/2019/09/theodore-mccarrick-archbishop-interview-kansas-sexual-abuse.html?utm_source=substack&utm_medium=email.

97 ***And when she asked who:*** Graham, "Theodore McCarrick."

97 *In his 2018 statement to the media:* Nicole Winfield, "McCarrick: What's Known About the Abusive US Ex-Cardinal," *AP News*, November 9, 2020, https://apnews.com/article/theodore-mccarrick-ex-cardinal-scandal-989fb97f4f0cad8c4926e8cb795ba2bf.

97 *"There were so many opportunities:* Sarah Rankin, "'It's Crushing': Survivors React to McCarrick Abuse Report," *AP News*, November 11, 2020, https://apnews.com/article/sexual-abuse-by-clergy-f9c8e7bfcfb21a5e9c05e680366f63bc.

97 *Maybe my life would:* Rankin, "'It's Crushing'."

97 *Geoffery Downs, who accused:* Rankin, "'It's Crushing'."

98 *How they could ever repair:* Rankin, "'It's Crushing'."

98 *DeVille, a Catholic, writes:* Adam A. J. DeVille, "Who Can We Forgive?" *Commonweal*, October 16, 2022, https://www.commonwealmagazine.org/forgiveness-mccarrick-church-abuse-psychotherapy.

98 *However, he says:* Deville, "Who Can We Forgive?"

98 *DeVille writes that as a psychologist:* Deville, "Who Can We Forgive?"

98 *"Good psychotherapy," DeVille writes:* Deville, "Who Can We Forgive?"

99 *Forgiveness breaks deathly cycles:* Deville, "Who Can We Forgive?"

Chapter 6

103 *According to then-current editor:* Daniel Silliman, "Sexual Harassment Went Unchecked at Christianity Today," *Christianity Today*, March 15, 2022, https://www.christianitytoday.com/news/2022/march/sexual-harassment-ct-guidepost-assessment-galli-olawoye.html.

104 *It has also been primarily led by men:* Rainn.org, "Victims of Sexual Violence: Statistics," accessed October 23, 2023, https://www.rainn.org/statistics/victims-sexual-violence.

105 *Boedy, who wrote about the pastor:* Matthew Boedy, "Disturbing Allegations of Spiritual Abuse at James Walden's Acts 29 Riverside Community Church in Columbia, South Carolina," *Wondering Eagle*, November 2, 2016, https://wonderingeagle.wordpress.com/2016/11/02/disturbing-allegations-of-spiritual-abuse-at-james-waldens-acts-29-riverside-community-church-in-columbia-south-carolina/.

105 *In an essay at the website:* David VanDrunen, "The Forgiveness of Sin," *The Gospel Coalition*, accessed October 23, 2023, https://www.thegospelcoalition.org/essay/the-forgiveness-of-sin/.

106 *According to writer and former:* Katelyn Beaty, "Christians Love a Good Comeback Story. Too Often It's Cheap Grace," *Religion & Politics*, September 27, 2022, https://religionandpolitics.org/2022/09/27/christians-love-a-comeback-story-too-often-its-cheap-grace/?utm_source=substack&utm_medium=email.

106 *The writer Elizabeth Spiers:* Elizabeth Spiers, "Jerry Falwell Jr. and the Evangelical Redemption Plot" *New York Review*, August 20, 2020, https://www.nybooks.com/online/2020/08/20/jerry-falwell-jr-and-the-evangelical-redemption-plot/.

106 *Among Evangelical laypeople:* Beaty, "Christians Love a Good Comeback."

107 *In one disturbing incident:* Silliman, "Sexual Harassment."

107 *Amy Jackson, a former associate:* Silliman, "Sexual Harassment."

107 *Guidepost Solutions, the consulting firm:* Silliman, "Sexual Harassment."

107 *For his part, Galli:* Bob Smietana, "Former Christianity Today Editor Mark Galli Accused of Sexual Harassment," *Religion News Service*, March 15, 2022, https://religionnews.com/2022/03/15/former-christianity-today-editor-mark-galli-accused-of-sexual-harassment-trump/.

108 *We owe it to the women:* Timothy Dalrymple, "We Fell Short in Protecting Our Employees," *Christianity Today*, March 15, 2022, https://www.christianitytoday.com/ct/2022/march-web-only/we-fell-short-in-protecting-our-employees-editorial.html.

109 *From an Evangelical perspective:* Molly Olmstead, "Investigating Sexual Harassment in an Evangelical Christian Newsroom," *Slate*, March 23, 2022, https://slate.com/news-and-politics/2022/03/christianity-today-reporter-sexual-harassment-investigation.html.

109 *Silliman goes on to say:* Olmstead, "Investigating Sexual Harassment."

109 *Back in 2003:* Peter Smith, "Catholic Bishop Criticizes Media," *The Courier-Journal*, September 6, 2003, https://www.poynter.org/reporting-editing/2003/catholic-bishop-criticizes-media/.

110 *In the Atlantic, Evangelical writer:* David French, "The Southern Baptist Horror," *Atlantic*, May 23, 2022, https://12ft.io/proxy?q=https%3A%2F%2Fwww.theatlantic.com%2Fideas%2Farchive%2F2022%2F05%2Fsouthern-baptist-evangelical-allegations-cover-up%2F629954%2F&utm_source=substack&utm_medium=email.

110 *The report also revealed that SBC:* French, "The Southern Baptist Horror."

110 *In June of 2020:* Daniel Lavery, @daniel_m_lavery, "In November of last year, I reported to the Elders of Menlo Church that their senior pastor, John Ortberg, had conspired in secret to provide a person experiencing compulsive sexual feelings towards children with unsupervised access to young people through youth groups," June 28, 2020, 4:39 PM, https://twitter.com/daniel_m_lavery/status/1277386063888166913.

111 *For Hybels and other megachurch:* Laurie Goldstein, "He's a Superstar Pastor. She Worked for Him and Says He Groped Her Repeatedly," *New York Times*, August 5, 2018, https://www.nytimes.com/2018/08/05/us/bill-hybels-willow-creek-pat-baranowski.html.

111 *And in megachurches independent:* Goldstein, "He's a Superstar Pastor."

112 *"Those leaders feel almost invincible":* Goldstein, "He's a Superstar Pastor."

112 *According to Bob Smietana's reporting:* Bob Smietana, "Megachurch Pastor John Ortberg Kept a Family Member's Attraction to Children a Secret. Then His Son Blew the Whistle," Religion News Service, July 6, 2020, https://religionnews.com/2020/07/06/megachurch-pastor-john-ortberg-family-member-attraction-to-children-secret-menlo-church-daniel-lavery-whistelblower/.

112 *He wrote to them:* Daniel Silliman, "John Ortberg's Church Says 'No Evidence of Misconduct' as More Details Emerge," *Christianity Today*, July 7, 2020, https://www.christianitytoday.com/news/2020/july/john-ortberg-lavery-menlo-investigation.html.

113 *Lavery expressed skepticism:* Silliman, "John Ortberg's Church."

113 *In the Twitter thread, Lavery:* Daniel Lavery, @daniel_m_lavery, ""parishioners were not given the full story of Ortberg's relationship to this volunteer, or his interest in keeping their strategy a secret," Twitter, June 28, 2020, 4:39 p.m.

113 *Ortberg admitted to using:* Fiona Kelliher, "Bay Area Megachurch Pastor Resigns Amid Scandal Fallout," *Mercury News*, July 29, 2020, https://www.mercurynews.com/2020/07/29/bay-area-megachurch-pastor-resigns-amid-scandal-fallout/.

113 *In his newsletter, Lavery wrote:* Daniel Lavery, "If Compelled to Abide: On Sobriety, Marriage, and Fictional Dog-Killing," *The Chatner* (newsletter), September 7, 2021, https://www.thechatner.com/p/if-compelled-to-abide-on-sobriety.

113 *Lavery told Vanity Fair that:* Claire Landsbaum, "Daniel M. Lavery Comes Unstuck," *Vanity Fair*, February 27, 2020, https://www.vanityfair.com/style/2020/02/daniel-lavery-comes-unstuck-something-that-may-shock-and-discredit-you.

113 *Lavery described the final conversation:* Daniel Lavery, "Thoughts on a Phone Call," *The Chatner* (newsletter), February 6, 2020, https://www.thechatner.com/p/thoughts-on-a-phone-call.

114 *As the Evangelical journalist Julie Roys:* Julie Roys, "John Ortberg and the Problem of Replatforming Leaders after Scandal," *The Roys Report*, February 2, 2022, https://julieroys.com/opinion-john-ortberg-problem-replatforming-leaders/.

115 *In her book Healing Spiritual Wounds:* Carol Howard Merritt, *Healing Spiritual Wounds: Reconnecting with a Loving God after Experiencing a Hurtful Church* (New York: HarperOne, 2017).

115 *Rev. Merritt explains that:* Carol Howard Merritt, in discussion with the author, 2017.

115 *In many cases, this is:* Merritt, discussion.

115 *Spiritual abuse can also:* Merritt, discussion.

115 *The aftermath experiences of victims:* Merritt, *Healing Spiritual Wounds.*

116 *In churches "where there's:* Katheryn Joyce, in discussion with the author, 2017.

116 *According to Joyce, in:* Joyce, discussion.

117 *Sarah Jones, who writes for:* Joyce, discussion.

117 *One way in which:* Merritt, discussion.

117 *Merritt explains that "this:* Merritt, discussion.

117 *In patriarchal churches:* Merritt, discussion.

118 Merritt, discussion.

118 *This patriarchal version:* Merritt, discussion.

118 *Joyce explains that for:* Joyce, discussion.

118 *Organizations like GRACE:* Joyce, discussion.

119 *And Sarah Jones adds that:* Joyce, discussion.

119 *In 2022, it was announced:* "Nice things People Say," *Embracing the Journey*, https://www.embracingthejourney.org/nice-things-people-say.html.

119 *Stanley stated that he wanted:* Ian M. Giatti, "Andy Stanley to Host Conference for Christian Parents of LGBT-Identified Kids," *Christian Post*, January 31, 2023, https://www.christianpost.com/news/andy-stanley-to-host-conference-for-christians-with-lgbt-kids.html.

120 *Lavery's response to the reader went:* Danny M. Lavery, "Help! My Brother Assaulted me. My Family Wants Me to Get Over It." *Slate*, March 26, 2019, https://slate.com/human-interest/2019/03/brother-assault-forgive-advice.html.

Chapter 7

121 *In Heather King's memoir:* Heather King, *Redeemed: Stumbling Toward God, Sanity, and the Peace That Passes All Understanding* (New York: Penguin, 2009).

122 *Many Rwandans are devout Catholics:* Guttmacher Institute, "Abortion in Rwanda," April 2013, https://www.guttmacher.org/fact-sheet/abortion-rwanda.

124 *At the time, he told Time magazine:* Andrew Downie, "Nine-Year-Old's Abortion Outrages Brazil's Catholic Church," *Time*, March 6, 2009, https://content.time.com/time/world/article/0,8599,1883598,00.html.

125 *For every person who joins:* Pew Research Center, "America's Changing Religious Landscape," May 12, 2015, https://www.pewresearch.org/religion/2015/05/12/chapter-2-religious-switching-and-intermarriage/.

125 *Thirty percent of Southern:* Bob Smietana, "Southern Baptists Lost Nearly Half a Million Members in 2022," *Religion News Service*, May 9, 2023.

126 *The days of enormous Catholic families:* Lisa McClian, "How the Catholic Church Came to Oppose Birth Control," *The Conversation*, July 9, 2018, https://theconversation.com/how-the-catholic-church-came-to-oppose-birth-control-95694#:~:text=Regarding%20his%20frank%201930%20pronouncement,a%20great%20and%20mortal%20flaw.%E2%80%9D.

126 *And given that studies show:* Elizabeth Dias, "'It Is Not a Closet. It Is a Cage.' Gay Catholic Priests Speak Out," *New York Times*, February 17, 2019, https://www.nytimes.com/2019/02/17/us/it-is-not-a-closet-it-is-a-cage-gay-catholic-priests-speak-out.html.

127 *According to Pew Research:* David Masci, "Most Americans Believe in Jesus' Virgin Birth," Pew Research Center, December 25, 2013, https://www.pewresearch.org/fact-tank/2013/12/25/most-americans-believe-in-jesus-virgin-birth/.

127 *He declares virginity "most excellent":* Aquinas, *Summa Theologica*.

128 *Aquinas further says that if a virgin:* Aquinas, *Summa Theologica*.

129 *At 3 p.m. on July 5, 1902, Maria Goretti:* "Maria Goretti—Saint under Siege," *Sunday Times*, accessed October 23, 2023, https://www.sundaytimes.lk/020707/plus/7.html.

129 *According to one biography that heaves:* Geofferey Poage, *St. Maria Goretti: In Garments All Red* (Charlotte, NC: Tan Books, 1988), 37.

129 *He lived until 1970:* "Alessandro Serenelli: A Miraculous Conversion," Mariagoretti.org, accessed October 23, 2023, http://www.mariagoretti.org/alessandrobio.htm.

129 *There is then in this world:* "Text of Pope's Homily at Canonization of Saint Maria Goretti," *Catholic Standard and Times*, June 30, 1950, https://thecatholicnewsarchive.org/?a=d&d=cst19500630-01.2.10&e=-------en-20--1--txt-txIN--------.

130 *Half a million people:* "An 11-Year-Old Girl Is Made a Saint," *Life Magazine*, July 17, 1950, https://books.google.com/books?id=fUoEAAAAMBAJ&lpg=PA107&dq=Maria%20Goretti%20outdoors&pg=PA107#v=onepage&q=Maria%20Goretti%20outdoors&f=false.

130 *The website listing the dates:* Pilgrimage of Mercy, "Saint Maria Goretti," accessed October 23, 2023, https://mariagoretti.com/#:~:text=While%20St.,a%20path%20to%20personal%20holiness.

130 *In Commonweal Magazine:* B. D. McClay, "Problems Like Maria," *Commonweal*, July 31, 2018, https://www.commonwealmagazine.org/problems-maria.

130 *After all, when she was canonized:* Stephen Robertson, "Age of Consent Laws," *Children & Youth in History*, accessed October 23, 2023, https://chnm.gmu.edu/cyh/teaching-modules/230.html.

131 *During Kelly's 2022 trial:* Erum Salam, "'You Destroyed So Many Lives': R Kelly Victims Give Emotional Statements," *The Guardian*, June 29, 2022, https://www.theguardian.com/us-news/2022/jun/29/r-kelly-victims-impact-statements.

132 *At the beatification Mass:* Cardinal Becciu, "Homily of the Prefect of the Congregation for the Causes of Saints for the Beatification of the Servant of God Anna Kolesárová, 01.09.2018," Holy See Press Office, accessed October 23, 2023, https://press.vatican.va/content/salastampa/en/bollettino/pubblico/2018/09/01/180901d.html.

132 *Like Maria Goretti, he continued:* Becciu, "Homily of the Prefect."

132 *The Slovak bishops further said:* Mollie Wilson O'Reilly, "Her, Too," *Commonweal*, September 17, 2018, https://www.commonwealmagazine.org/her-too.

133 *In it, Denhollander says:* Rachel Denhollander. "My Larry Nassar Testimony Went Viral. But There's More to the Gospel Than Forgiveness," *Christianity Today*, January 13, 2018, https://www.christianitytoday.com/ct/2018/january-web-only/rachael-denhollander-larry-nassar-forgiveness-gospel.html.

133 *However, according to Denhollander:* Denhollander. "My Larry Nassar Testimony."

133 *In her victim impact statement:* "Read Rachel Denhollander's Full Victim Impact Statement about Larry Nassar," *CNN*, January 30, 2018, https://www.cnn.com/2018/01/24/us/rachael-denhollander-full-statement/.

134 *The suffering here on earth:* "Read Rachel Denhollander's."

134 *Biles told the Senate:* Rev.com, "Testimony on Larry Nassar Abuse Investigation: Opening Statement Transcript," September 15, 2021, https://www.rev.com/blog/transcripts/simone-biles-testimony-on-larry-nassar-abuse-investigation-opening-statement-transcript.

134 *She told the Senate:* Rev.com, "Testimony on Larry Nassar."

134 *But Denhollander says that:* Denhollander, "My Larry Nassar Testimony."

135 *Nassar said to the abuse victims:* Raj Persaud, "Larry Nassar and the Psychology of the Insincere Apology," *Psychology Today* (blog), January 26, 2018, https://www.psychologytoday.com/us/blog/slightly-blighty/201801/larry-nassar-and-the-psychology-the-insincere-apology.

135 *In one psychological study:* Persaud, "Larry Nassar."

136 *"Obedience," she told Christianity Today:* Denhollander, "My Larry Nassar Testimony."

136 *As Molly O'Reilly writes:* O'Reilly, "Her, Too."

137 *According to sociologist Anson Shupe:* Rachel Walter Goosen, "Defanging the Beast: Mennonite Responses to John Howard Yoder's Sexual Abuse,"

Bishop Accountability.org, https://www.bishop-accountability.org/news5/2015_01_Goossen_Defanging_the_Beast.pdf.

137 *Yoder went through seven rounds:* Goosen, "Defanging the Beast."

138 *Florer-Bixler says that:* Melissa Florer-Bixler *How to Have an Enemy: Righteous Anger and the Work of Peace* (Harrisonburg, VA: Herald Press, 2021).

138 *B. D. McClay writes that the women:* McClay, "Problems Like Maria."

138 *Carolyn Holderread Heggen, one:* Goosen, "Defanging the Beast."

138 *Nonetheless, Yoder emerged from:* Mark Oppenheimer, "A Theologian's Influence, and Stained Past, Live On," *New York Times*, October 11, 2013, https://www.nytimes.com/2013/10/12/us/john-howard-yoders-dark-past-and-influence-lives-on-for-mennonites.html?pagewanted=all.

138 *Yoder was welcomed back:* Oppenheimer, "A Theologian's Influence."

139 *Nelson Kraybill, the president of:* Quoted in Goosen, "Defanging the Beast."

139 *And at the end of Yoder's:* Goosen, "Defanging the Beast."

139 *The Catholic theologian Andrew Greely:* Goosen, "Defanging the Beast."

140 *The lament included these lines:* Anabaptist Mennonite Biblical Seminary, "AMBS Response to Victims of John H. Yoder Abuse," https://www.ambs.edu/ambs-response-to-victims-of-john-howard-yoder-abuse/.

142 *In order for a person to incur:* The Holy See, "Nuovo Libro VI del Codice di Diritto Canonico, 01.06.2021," June 1, 2021, https://press.vatican.va/content/salastampa/it/bollettino/pubblico/2021/06/01/0348/00750.html#in.

143 *Although beliefs about:* Garry Wills, "The Bishops Are Wrong about Biden—And Abortion," *New York Times*, June 27, 2021, https://www.nytimes.com/2021/06/27/opinion/biden-bishops-communion-abortion.html.

Chapter 8

147 *"For such a one," he wrote:* 2 Cor 2:5–11, NIV.

147 *As one contemporary pastor said:* Mark Driscoll, "Forgiveness Disarms the Demonic," *Patheos* (blog), November 5, 2019, https://www.patheos.com/blogs/markdriscoll/2019/11/forgiveness-disarms-the-demonic/.

147 *The pastor who wrote this was:* Michael Paulson, "A Brash Style That Filled Pews, Until Followers Had Their Fill," New York Times, August 22, 2014, https://www.nytimes.com/2014/08/23/us/mark-driscoll-is-being-urged-to-leave-mars-hill-church.html.

148 *Using the online pseudonym:* Matthew Paul Turner, "Mark Driscoll's Pussified Nation," *Matthew Paul Turner* (blog), July 29, 2014, https://matthewpaulturner.com/2014/07/29/mark-driscolls-pussified-nation/.

148 *Driscoll was known to scream:* Paulson, "A Brash Style."

148 *In his apology letter to the church:* "Mark Driscoll Posts an Open Letter of Apology," *Relevant*, March 17, 2014, https://relevantmagazine.com/faith/mark-driscoll-posts-open-letter-apology/.

148 *After enormous public pressure:* Kate Shellnutt, "Former Mars Hill Elders: Mark Driscoll Is Still 'Unrepentant,' Unfit to Pastor," *Christianity Today*, July 26, 2021, https://www.christianitytoday.com/news/2021/july/mars-hill-elders-letter-mark-driscoll-pastor-resign-trinity.html.

149 *For people in recovery:* Alcoholics Anonymous, "The Twelve Steps," https://www.aa.org/the-twelve-steps.

150 *The psychologist Matt James writes:* Matt James, "How to Forgive Yourself," *Psychology Today*, January 2022, https://www.psychologytoday.com/us/articles/202201/how-forgive-yourself.

150 *Narcissism, which the Diagnostic:* https://www.ncbi.nlm.nih.gov/books/NBK556001/.

150 *Sociopaths, who "habitually:* David Porter and Christie Hunter, "Antisocial Personality Disorder DSM-5 301.7 (F60.2)," *Theravive*, accessed October 23, 2023, https://www.theravive.com/therapedia/antisocial-personality-disorder-dsm--5-301.7-(f60.2).

151 *She writes that these:* Peg O'Connor, quoted in James, "How to Forgive Yourself."

151 *Every act confirms your inadequacy:* Peg O'Connor, quoted in James, "How to Forgive Yourself."

151 *You believe everything you do:* Peg O'Connor, quoted in James, "How to Forgive Yourself."

151 *The writer Anneli Rufus says:* Anneli S. Rufus, "The Most Painful Emotion," *Psychology Today*, January 2022, https://www.psychologytoday.com/us/articles/202201/how-forgive-yourself.

153 *While rituals and sacrifices:* Candida Moss, "How Christianity Co-Opted Yom Kippur to Explain Jesus' Death," *Daily Beast*, October 9, 2019, https://www.thedailybeast.com/how-christianity-co-opted-yom-kippur-to-explain-jesus-death.

154 *The writer Blake Chastain:* Bradley Onishi, "The Rise of #Exvangelical," *Religion & Politics*, April 19, 2019, https://religionandpolitics.org/2019/04/09/the-rise-of-exvangelical/.

155 *In 2018, as the deconstruction:* Andreea Nica, "The Forgotten Nones: The High Cost of Fleeing Fundamentalist Religion," *Religion Dispatches*, March 12, 2018, https://religiondispatches.org/the-forgotten-nones-the-high-cost-of-fleeing-fundamentalist-religion/.

156 *Westover wrote in her memoir:* Tara Westover, *Educated: A Memoir* (New York: Random House, 2018).

156 *Her parents' religion, she said:* Michelle Garrett Bulsiewicz, "Q&A: BYU Grad and 'Educated' Author Tara Westover Talks Difference between

Forgiveness and Reconciliation," *Deseret News*, March 20, 2018, https://www.deseret.com/2018/3/20/20642049/q-a-byu-grad-and-educated-author-tara-westover-talks-difference-between-forgiveness-and-reconciliati.

159 *He led a megachurch:* Carly Mayberry, "Josh Harris Launches Course on Deconstructing Faith, but Some Theologians Question His Motives," Newsweek, August 13, 2021, https://www.newsweek.com/josh-harris-launches-course-deconstructing-faith-some-theologians-question-his-motives-1619263.

159 *Harris's website also included:* Mayberry, "Josh Harris Launches Course."

159 *Ultimately, Harris ended up:* Jessica Leah, "UPDATE: After 'Valid Criticism,' Josh Harris Takes Down His Deconstruction Course," *ChurchLeaders.com*, August 16, 2021, https://churchleaders.com/news/403209-joshua-harris-deconstruction-course.html.

161 *For his founding of L'Arche:* Colleen Dulle, "Jean Varnier, 'Living Saint' Who Ministered to People with Disabilities, Dies at 90," *America Magazine*, May 27, 2019, https://www.americamagazine.org/faith/2019/05/07/jean-vanier-living-saint-who-ministered-people-disabilities-dies-90.

161 *Less than a year after Vanier's death:* "L'Arche Founder Jean Varnier Sexually Abused Women—Internal Report," *BBC News*, February 22, 2020, https://www.bbc.com/news/world-51596516.

161 *Before he himself was accused:* "Catholic Charity Founder Sexually Abused Women, Says Report," *Guardian*, February 22, 2020, https://www.theguardian.com/world/2020/feb/22/larche-founder-jean-vanier-sexually-abused-women-says-report.

161 *Phillipe had long been an abuser:* Céline Hoyeau, "L'Arche fait la lumière sur la face cachée du P. Thomas Philippe," *La Croix*, October 15, 2015, https://www.la-croix.com/Religion/Actualite/L-Arche-fait-la-lumiere-sur-la-face-cachee-du-P.-Thomas-Philippe-2015-10-15-1368960.

162 *According to the report:* Bernard Granger, Nicole Jeammet, florian Michel, Antoine Mourges, Gwennola Rimbaut, and Claire Vincent-Mory, *Control and Abuse Investigation on Thomas Philippe, Jean Varnier and L'Arche (1950–2019)* (Study Commission Mandated by L'Arche Foundation: January 2023), 827, https://commissiondetude-jeanvanier.org/commission-detudeindependante2023-empriseetabus/wp-content/uploads/2023/01/Report_Control-and-Abuse_EN.pdf.

162 *As for Vanier, a recollection:* Granger et al., *Control and Abuse.*

162 *This person goes on to say:* "Control and Abuse," 708.

163 *This included "spiritual deviation":* Mitchell Atencio, "Jean Vanier Began L'Arche to Cover Abusive 'Mystical-Sexual' Practices, Finds Report," *Sojourners*, January 30, 2023, https://sojo.net/articles/jean-vanier-began-l-arche-cover-abusive-mystical-sexual-practices-finds-report.

163 *Vanier continued to use his Atencio:* "Jean Vanier Began L'Arche."

164 *A British medical journal that:* Mark Woods, "Mother Teresa and Her Critics: Should She Really Be Made a Saint?" *Christianity Today*, August 31, 2018, https://www.christiantoday.com/article/mother-teresa-and-her-critics-should-she-really-be-made-a-saint/94365.htm.

164 *Canadian doctors who did a follow-up:* Woods, "Mother Teresa."

165 *It's well reported that she:* Daniel Trotta, "Letters Reveal Mother Teresa's Doubt about Faith," Reuters, August 4, 2007, https://www.reuters.com/article/us-teresa-letters/letters-reveal-mother-teresas-doubt-about-faith-idUSN2435506020070824.

165 *Charles was dressed as a Texas Ranger:* Jenna Barnett, "Episode 1: The Second Death of Jean Varnier," January 24, 2023, in *Lead Us Not*, produced by Betsy Shirley, podcast, https://sojo.net/media/episode-1-second-death-jean-vanier.

166 *Barnett: If you could talk to the survivors:* Barnett, "Episode 1."

167 *In the Reddit sub for people:* u/regretfulperson11, "How to Forgive Yourself after Being Abused?" January 11, 2017, 5:06 a.m., Reddit post, https://www.reddit.com/r/BPD/comments/5nbtgn/how_to_forgive_yourself_after_being_abuse/.

167 *They went on to say:* u/regretfulperson11, "How to Forgive Yourself."

167 *Its website cheerfully declares:* "Founders," Trinity Church, accessed October 23, 2023, https://thetrinitychurch.com/our-leadership/.

Chapter 9

170 *Forgiveness, she said, is something:* Rodrigo Perez, "'Women Talking' Director Sarah Polley Developing a Film Inspired by Her Awards Season Run," *The Playlist*, March 13, 2023, https://theplaylist.net/women-talking-director-sarah-polley-on-forgiveness-the-guiding-principles-of-her-acclaimed-new-drama-20230112/.

170 *What you were required:* Perez, "'Women Talking'."

170 *Ona, who is pregnant:* Perez, "'Women Talking'."

171 *I believe those women because:* Rebecca Mead, "Sarah Polley's Journey from Child Star to Feminist Auteur," *New Yorker*, November 14, 2022, https://www.newyorker.com/magazine/2022/11/21/sarah-polleys-journey-from-child-star-to-feminist-auteur.

172 *Sarah Polley said a pivotal:* Perez, "'Women Talking'."

173 *While depictions of a person:* StrategyOne, *Survey of Love and Forgiveness in American Society*, Fetzer Institute, October 2010, https://fetzer.org/sites/default/files/images/resources/attachment/%5Bcurrent-date%3Atiny%5D/Survey%20of%20Love%20and%20Forgiveness%20in%20American%20Society%20Report.pdf.

173 *The program assists about:* "Our Founder Father Greg," Homeboy Industries, accessed October 23, 2023, https://homeboyindustries.org/our-story/father-greg/.

173 *Boyle writes that:* Greg Boyle, *Forgive Everyone Everything* (Chicago: Loyola Press, 2022).

175 *Maimonides's first step toward:* Ruttenberg, *On Repentance and Repair*, 27.

175 *They then have to offer:* Ruttenberg, *On Repentance and Repair*, 41.

175 *The final step, and the one perhaps:* Ruttenberg, *On Repentance and Repair*, 43.

176 *But a problem in our typical:* Ruttenberg, *On Repentance and Repair*, 57.

176 *But "we as a society":* Ruttenberg, *On Repentance and Repair*, 90.

177 *Negest Rucker, a descendant of:* Annalisa Merelli, "The Jesuits' Plan to Compensate Their Slaves' Descendants Gets Reparation Wrong," *Quartz*, June 3, 2021, https://qz.com/2010943/georgetown-and-the-jesuits-slavery-reparations-plan-falls-short.

177 *"After the money has been paid":* Ruttenberg, *On Repentance and Repair*, 113.

177 *"In fact," according to Ruttenberg:* Ruttenberg, *On Repentance and Repair*, 186.

178 *Roof wrote a white supremacist:* Alan Blinder and Kevin Sack, "Dylann Roof, Addressing Court, Offers No Apology or Explanation for Massacre," *New York Times*, January 4, 2017, https://www.nytimes.com/2017/01/04/us/dylann-roof-sentencing.html.

179 *Who has been hurt?:* Howard Zehr, *Changing Lenses—A New Focus for Crime and Justice*, 3rd ed. (Scottdale, PA: Herald Press, 2005), 271.

179 *Zehr says that for proponents:* Howard Zehr. "Restorative Justice. What's That?" *Zehr Institute for Restorative Justice*, accessed October 23, 2023, https://zehr-institute.org/what-is-rj/.

179 *According to Zehr:* Zehr, "Restorative Justice."

180 *Lindsay Pointer, the associate director:* Lindsey Pointer, "What Is 'Restorative Justice' and How Does It Impact Individuals Involved in Crime?" *BJA NTTAC National Training and Technical Assistance Center* (blog), August 5, 2021, https://bjatta.bja.ojp.gov/media/blog/what-restorative-justice-and-how-does-it-impact-individuals-involved-crime.

180 *As Pointer writes:* Pointer, "What Is 'Restorative Justice.'"

181 *Like much of what locals call:* "DataQuest," California Department of Education, accessed October 23, 2023, https://data1.cde.ca.gov/dataquest/.

181 *and the neighborhood has the:* Da Lin, "Despite Some Neighborhood Spikes, Violent Crime in Oakland Declined in '22," *CBS News Bay Area*, December 11, 2022, https://www.cbsnews.com/sanfrancisco/news/despite-neighborhood-spikes-violent-crime-oakland-decline/.

181 *1 in 3 students:* Carolyn Jones, "At This Oakland High School, Restorative Justice Goes Far Beyond Discipline," *EdSource*, June 16, 2022,

https://edsource.org/2022/at-this-oakland-high-school-restorative-justice-goes-far-beyond-discipline/673453.

181 *On Fremont High's restorative justice:* "Restorative Justice at Fremont High School, Oakland CA," OUSD.org, accessed October 23, 2023, https://sites.google.com/ousd.org/rj-at-fremont/.

181 *School leaders write that in:* "Restorative Justice at Fremont High."

182 *Today, according to Tatiana Chaterji:* Jones, "At This Oakland High School."

182 *Fremont High students also now teach:* Jones, "At This Oakland High School."

182 *It read, in part, that:* Sam Levin, "'Unsung Hero': The Baker and Activist Whose Death Inspired Calls for Restorative Justice," *Guardian*, February 18, 2023, https://www.theguardian.com/us-news/2023/feb/18/jen-angel-oakland-baker-angel-cakes.

183 *People on Twitter said anything:* NorCal Independent (@209Independent), "So they are indirectly endorsing the next criminal act of this kind. Very sad, and disappointing. Sure wish these Liberals would grow a back bone." Twitter, February 10, 2023, 10:18 a.m., https://twitter.com/209Independent/status/1624095568682446848.

183 *to arguing that:* https://twitter.com/noBS49ers/status/162484872509614 8992.

183 *According to Mottley, Angel:* Brooke Anderson, "Jen Angel Wanted to Abolish Police and Prisons. She Wouldn't Want Her Death to Be Used to Incarcerate Anyone," *In These Times*, March 9, 2023, https://inthesetimes.com/article/jen-angel-abolition-mariame-kaba-oakland.

185 *Toward the end of her book:* Jeanne Safer, *Forgiving and Not Forgiving* (New York: Quill, 2000).

185 *Safer expands on this further:* Safer, *Forgiving and Not Forgiving*, 203–4.